AVARICVM

A Latin Text of Caesar's *Gallic War* VII 1–28

with Running Vocabulary and Commentary

John Lanier

Elizabeth Cross

Katherine Cross

Lian E

Zachary Shepherd Haarz

Fiona Lee

Peter Olmeda

Clara Grey Peters

Marilia Chiu Serôdio

PIXELIA PUBLISHING

Latin Editions Editors:

Thomas G. Hendrickson

John Lanier

Anna C. Pisarello

pixeliapublishing.org

AVARICVM: A Latin Text of Caesar's *Gallic War* VII 1-28

with Running Vocabulary and Commentary

First Edition

Copyright © 2023 Pixelia Publishing

Use of this work is governed by a Creative Commons BY-NC-SA License. The terms of the license can be accessed at creativecommons.org/licenses/by-nc-sa/4.0/.

Accordingly, you are free to copy, alter, and distribute this work freely under the following conditions:

(1) You must attribute this work to the authors (but not in any way that suggests that the authors endorse any alterations you make to the work).

(2) You may not use this work for commercial purposes.

(3) If you alter, transform, or build upon this work, you must distribute the resulting work only under the same or similar license as this one.

ISBN: 978-1-7370330-3-5

Published 2023 by Pixelia Publishing (Williamsburg, VA, USA)

pixeliapublishing.org

Illustrations by Suran Gao and Evan Kim

Font: Cardo, an open source font in the Google Fonts collection, designed by David Perry
Maps and cover design by John Lanier. Front: Obverse of a silver denarius of 48 BCE depicting a Gallic shield and a bearded Gaul, probably Vercingetorix; American Numismatic Society, ref. RRC 448/2a, identifier 1937.158.248 Back: an anthropomorphic Celtic sword type ca. 60 BCE in the Metropolitan Museum of Art, Accession Number 1999.94a-d

CONTENTS

ILLUSTRATIONS

ABOUT THIS EDITION

This book is the culmination of student work in the advanced Latin course at Stanford Online High School in the academic year 2022-2023. It is the first of three planned books covering Caesar's *dē bellō Gallicō* VII. The content of Pixelia volumes is generated primarily by the students and is meant to aid intermediate Latin learners in reading texts without the need to constantly consult separate dictionaries and commentaries. John Lanier taught the course and devised the division of Book VII into three parts, such that each part was of the appropriate length for the students to complete in one academic year and roughly equivalent in content. AVARICVM includes chapters 1-28, roughly 3,700 words, covering the events of Book VII up to the fall of Avaricum. The second volume (GERGOVIA; chapters 29-62, ca. 4,400 words) and third volume (ALESIA: chapters 63-90, ca. 3,600 words) will follow in subsequent years.

The student editors of AVARICVM were Elizabeth Cross, Katherine Cross, Lian E, Zachary Shepherd Haarz, Fiona Lee, Peter Olmeda, Clara Grey Peters, and Marilia Chiu Serôdio. We subdivided the text of Chapters 1-28 such that each student was the editor of their own section of ca. 400 words. As a first task, the students developed working translations of their sections in order to get a sense of the Latin and the basic narrative; they next developed the on-page vocabulary glosses; they then added and revised macrons[1] for all Latin text and vocabulary; and, finally, each student wrote explanatory commentary. The students

[1] The macrons were added through a web app (alatius.com/macronizer), which is highly accurate but does require occasional corrections.

were peer reviewers for each other at each step of the process, with Lanier as supervisor, final revisor, cartographer, and Introduction author.

Caesar has been a staple of Latin classrooms for centuries. His language is relatively straight-forward for beginners, and even in his own day it was a model for good Latin style (see, e.g., Cicero *Brutus* 262). Yet we should not take canonical status for granted, and in Caesar's case re-examination is particularly warranted. The *Gallic War*, for all its good style, was written as a justification for imperialism; or at least, the book was written about an imperial conquest, by the general carrying out that conquest, who presumably wrote it in a way that he thought would resonate with his audience back home. As for the book's traditional place in Latin classrooms over the last few centuries: it might well have had a certain appeal in early modern nations, like Britain and France, which had their own ambitions of imperial expansion. These same reasons might make Caesar less appealing today. And yet, *Gallic War* is an interesting and important text for students not despite this history but because of it.

Gallic War is a valuable witness to imperial expansion and its justification. In the space of a few hundred years, Rome grew from a village in central Italy to an empire encompassing nearly the whole Mediterranean world. What did Romans think of this expansion? How did Roman leaders justify it? Caesar's *Gallic War* provides a glimpse. Interestingly, it is not a text that downplays the violence of empire, nor does it show conquest to be an unalloyed good. It is Caesar himself who writes that at the sack of Avaricum, his troops massacred 40,000 inhabitants, sparing "not the elderly, nor women, nor children" (7.28.4). Though Caesar's commentaries are sometimes dismissed as self-aggrandizing propaganda, he often presents a Gallic perspective which is sympathetic and complex:

Book VII is filled with Caesar's observations about his opponents' motivations, and he frequently presents Gallic speech, or at least what he supposes Gallic speeches to contain: the Gauls are cunning, creative, brave, tenacious, patriotic, but also self-serving, greedy, fractious, and impetuous—in other words, very much like Caesar's peers back in Rome.

This complexity is particularly evident in Book VII, which narrates the final attempt of the Gauls to fight for their freedom under the leadership of the Gallic chieftain Vercingetorix. He is, for Caesar, the Gallic Hannibal or Mithridates, a brilliant and charismatic leader who is able, for perhaps the first time, to fully marshal the latent strength of a united Gaul and oppose Caesar on something like equal footing. He rallies the Gauls with impassioned calls for *lībertās*, a value which Romans held dearly (7.4.4). *Gallic War* Book VII is an ideal text for students because it allows them to experience, in Latin, a pivotal moment in history from the complex perspective of one of its chief actors.

The current book was born out of Lanier's wish to read Caesar's *Gallic War* VII selections with students in the advanced Latin course several years ago. At that time, options for a modern edition of *BG* VII with running commentary (in English) were quite limited, the most notable being Whiteley's "blue" Bristol edition. This book is sometimes difficult to acquire new, and the price of secondary copies is often prohibitive. In addition, Lanier felt the commentary to be somewhat sparse for Latin readers at the advanced high school level and wanted same-page vocabulary and commentary (on the model of Pharr's *Aeneid* or Geoffrey Steadman's excellent Greek and Latin editions, to which paradigm previous Pixelia editions have also adhered). Steadman has put out an edition of *BG* I and an edition of selections of Caesar in his *College Caesar* (though the latter does not draw from *BG* VII). It is our hope that this book, along with the two subsequent volumes, will serve as an accessible and useful guide in reading the lengthy and often difficult seventh book of Caesar's *Gallic War*.

Because Pixelia volumes are student-focused and truly collaborative, we have always felt that a shared byline of authors was most appropriate (even if unwieldy), and we continue that practice here. All the work in this volume was collaborative, with a special nod to Zachary Shepherd Haarz for penning Appendix C: the Roman Sacking of Cities. We give special thanks to Tom Hendrickson for developing the idea of Pixelia, designing the class, and supervising Pixelia's first two Latin volumes (*The Passion of Perpetua* and *Isotta Nogarola's Defense of Eve*). We are indebted to OHS students Lorelei Wright for managing the book's art and design choices, and to Suran Gao for the illustrations, with an additional half-page illustration by Evan Kim (p.37). OHS instructors Tom Hendrickson, Caedmon Haas, Ben Wiebracht, and Anna Pisarello provided valuable grammatical insight and editorial advice. We would also like to thank Tomohiro Hoshi (Head of School, Stanford Online High School), Josh Carlson (Director of Business Operations), and Christine Van Winkle (Associate Director of Business Operations) for their continued support of the Pixelia project. Prof. Randy Souza provided valuable advice in the selection of the perfect coin for the front cover.

The Latin text in this volume comes from the Loeb edition of 1919, in consultation with the Oxford Classical Text and its *apparatus criticus*. We have made no substantial changes to the text and encountered no major textual difficulties in these first 28 chapters of *BG* VII.

INTRODUCTION

BG VII in context

In the winter of 53 BCE, Caesar crossed the Alps back into northern Italy with a sense that Gaul was finally *quiēta,* if not *pācāta*. He had been waging war there for over five years already. The conflict had begun as a swift preventative action against the Helvetii as they attempted to move their entire tribe through the territory of the Roman province of *Gallia Trānsalpīna*. Caesar's defensive action, at the very beginning of his tenure in *Gallia Trānsalpīna*, steadily transformed into a campaign of conquest and subjugation which stretched far beyond the boundaries of his province. During those five years his force had grown to ten legions, some 50,000 soldiers all told. They had battled across Gaul numerous times on land and sea, ventured to Britain, bridged the Rhine twice, and withstood several serious challenges to the incremental establishment of Roman domination.

A year earlier, in 54 BCE, the most recent of these "rebellions," a surprise attack by the Gallic champion Ambiorix, had killed thousands of Roman soldiers and two of Caesar's most trusted lieutenants. He responded swiftly and severely with the widespread devastation of the lands of those he held responsible, as well as the summary execution of the Gallic leader Acco (*BG* 6.44; 7.1). He hoped that these harsh measures would finally end Gallic resistance to what must have seemed to him to be inevitable: the organization of the vast Gallic territory he had seized into Roman provincial possessions. As he returned to northern Italy to attend to his gubernatorial tasks at the end of 53, his attention was surely already turning to the details of this process, and also to the simmering political turmoil back in Rome, about which he makes brief mention in the opening chapter of Book VII. He had no way of knowing, as the new year began and as the miles grew between himself and his legions back in winter camps in central Gaul, that the Gallic tribes were not *quiētī* by any means and would soon explode with their final and most desperate bid for *lībertās*.

Book VII of *Gallic War* chronicles this final struggle of the Gauls against Roman domination. It begins, as was typical for these Gallic uprisings, with the leaders of the tribes holding a secret meeting. In past years, many had instigated uprisings and had been cast down by Caesar's reprisal: the Belgae in 57, the Veneti in 56, the Morini in 55, Ambiorix and his Eburones and then Indutiomarus and his Treveri in 54, Acco and the Senones in 53. This time, the instigator is the Carnutes tribe, and the epicenter is their chief town, Cenabum, where they slaughter a number of unsuspecting Roman businessmen. These *negōtiātōrēs* had no doubt been busy with the various tasks of converting Gaul into a productive Roman possession: organizing slave routes, assessing mining potential, surveying arable land. Now their slaying became Caesar's justification for the wrathful campaign which follows. Cenabum's inhabitants will experience Roman retribution (see Appendix C), but not before the uprising begun by the Carnutes had spread to a powerful coalition of tribes led by the Arverni and their electric and effective new leader, Vercingetorix, who promises *lībertās commūnis* from Roman *servitūs* for all the Gauls (7.4.4).

For a detailed introduction to Gaul, Caesar, and *Gallic War*, consult the excellent open-access Web Essays[2] provided as part of the *Landmark Julius Caesar*, edited and translated by Kurt A. Raaflaub (New York: Pantheon Books, 2017). In particular, students new to *Gallic War* will find useful: *Gaul in Caesar's Time* by O. Büchsenschütz; Oppida: *Towns in Caesar's World* by I. Ralston; *Late Republican Provincial Administration* by N. Rosenstein; *The Roman Army Camp* by D.B. Campbell; *Military Engineering and Sieges* by D.B. Campbell; *Military Logistics* by N. Rosenstein; *Caesar the General and Leader* by L. De Blois; and *The Roman* Commentarius *and Caesar's Commentaries* by K.A. Raaflaub.

Timeline of events for *Gallic War* I–VI (all dates are BCE)

BOOK I

1.1–5 (61-Spring 58): The Helvetii are persuaded by Orgetorix, an ambitious Helvetian leader, to migrate from their country. They burn their homes and prepare for a long journey.

1.6–9 (Mar-April 58): The Helvetii try to pass through the Roman Province on their migration, but Caesar prevents them. They instead pass through the territory of the Sequani.

1.10–15 (April-June 58): Caesar grows concerned about the Helvetian migration and decides to intervene, pursuing the Helvetii on their march. The Helvetii harass the Romans.

1.16–20 (June 58): Caesar learns from Liscus, the chief official of the Aedui, that Dumnorix has been building an opposing faction within the Aedui to undermine Roman influence. Caesar places him under guard.

[2] Visit thelandmarkcaesar.com

1.21–29 (June–July 58): Caesar launches an attack against the Helvetii. After a difficult battle, the Helvetii surrender, and Caesar pursues and captures a group of Helvetian runaways.

1.30–36 (July–Aug 58): Gallic emissaries come to thank Caesar and hold a Gallic council, led by the druid Diviciacus. He informs Caesar that the German king, Ariovistus, has settled in Sequani territory, and the Gauls need Roman assistance. Caesar promises his help and exchanges messages with the hostile Ariovistus, who does not respond to his warnings.

1.37–45 (Aug–Sep 58): The Romans advance towards Ariovistus. Caesar and Ariovistus meet, each with a group of cavalry; Caesar reiterates his demands, which Ariovistus again refuses.

1.46–50 (Sep 58): After the German horsemen attack Caesar during the parley, hostilities ensue. Caesar leaves his forces in battle formation, but Ariovistus declines to fight a decisive battle.

1.51–54 (Sep–Oct 58): Caesar forces the Germans to react by closely approaching their camp. The two armies clash, and the Germans flee to the Rhine; Ariovistus escapes. Caesar leads his army to winter quarters among the Sequani.

BOOK II

2.1–4 (Winter 58–July 57): Caesar learns that the Belgae are plotting against the Romans and joins his army at Vesontio, an *oppidum* of the Sequani. The Remi, one of the Belgae tribes, surrender to Caesar.

2.5–11 (July–Aug 57): Caesar saves the Remi *oppidum* of Bibrax from an attack by the Belgae and they make a camp nearby. The Romans and Belgae do battle, and after suffering heavy losses, the Belgae decide to return home; the Romans pursue and slaughter them.

2.12–14 (Aug 57): Caesar leads his army to Noviodunum, the capital of the Suessiones. The Suessiones surrender, followed by the Bellovaci and the Ambiani.

2.15–18 (Aug 57): The Nervii, neighbors of the Ambiani, resent the other Belgae for surrendering, and lie in wait for the Romans across the Sabis River.

2.19–28 (Aug–Sep 57): Caesar leads a difficult battle against the courageous Nervii. Following a decisive Roman victory, the Nervii women and elders surrender, and Caesar treats them with mercy.

2.29–33 (Sep–Oct 57): The Atuatuci, who were on their way to assist the Nervii, move everything to a single fortified town, where they are besieged by the Romans. Caesar agrees to spare them if they give up their weapons; they agree, but only give up two-thirds of their weapons. After a failed sortie, they are defeated and sold into slavery.

2.34–35 (Oct–Nov 57): Caesar learns that the maritime Gauls have surrendered to his legate, Crassus. He declares that all of Gaul has been pacified and sends his legions to winter quarters; the Roman Senate decrees a fifteen-day public thanksgiving.

BOOK III

3.1–6 (Sep–Nov 57): After the legate Galba opens a safe route through the Alps, the Gauls attack at Octodorus. The Romans kill a third of the 30,000 Gauls with a final charge.

3.7–16 (Dec 57–Sep 56): The maritime Veneti tribe takes Roman officials hostage; other tribes follow suit. After a meeting with the other triumvirs Pompey and Crassus in northern Italy, Caesar hurries to the western

Gallic coast. He orders a fleet to be built and sends legates with forces to stop the troubles from spreading. He then defeats the Veneti on the sea and punishes them.

3.17–19 (July–Sep 56 BC): Caesar sends the legate Sabinus against the Venelli. He defeats them after baiting them to attack by feigning cowardice. The entire region surrenders.

3.20–22 (Aug–Sep 56 BC): The Sotiates attack the legate Crassus, but quickly surrender. The enemy commander Adiatunnus attacks separately but he soon surrenders as well.

3.23–27 (Sep 56 BC): Crassus then sets out against the Vocates and Tarusates, and after storming their camp kills many. Most of Aquitania surrenders to Crassus.

3.28–29 (Oct–Nov 56 BC): Caesar is unsuccessful in catching the last remaining tribes, the Morini and Menapii. He burns their crops and buildings before sending the legions to their winter camps.

BOOK IV

4.1–11 (Dec–Jun 55 BC)**:** Caesar responds to German incursions into Gaul; he attempts negotiations.

4.12–15 (May–Jun 55 BC): The Germans attack Caesar's unsuspecting army. Caesar leads the legions to the enemy camp and slaughters them.

4.16–19 (Jun–Jul 55 BC): Caesar builds a bridge across the Rhine, then crosses into Germania to destroy Sugambri territory and help the Ubii. After eighteen days he returns and dismantles the bridge.

4.20–27 (Jul–Sep 55 BC): Caesar decides to cross to Britain and gives his reasons. He assembles two legions and cavalry, but the cavalry get separated and do not arrive in Britain. The Romans force a landing against the resistance of the Britons on a beach overlooked by cliffs;

though they struggle in the deep water at first, the legions quickly defeat the Britons once they are able to assemble on the beach.

4.28–36 (Sep-Oct 55 BC): The Roman ships are destroyed in a storm. Seeing this, the Britons violate their surrender terms and launch a surprise attack. Caesar is prepared and defeats them again. His soldiers manage to salvage some of the wrecked ships and the Romans limp back to Gaul.

4.37–38 (Oct 55 BC): Roman cavalry saves some errant legionnaires from the Morini, then the legate Labienus defeats the Morini and ravages their territory. The legions go into winter camps and the Roman Senate decrees a twenty-day thanksgiving for the exploits of the year.

BOOK V

5.1–7 (Jan-July 54): Caesar resolves to return to Britain in force. He deals with Gallic factional strife while his legions build ships at his instruction. The fleet's departure from Portus Itius is delayed by bad weather; meanwhile he orders many of the Gallic *principēs* to accompany him to Britain. Dumnorix the Aeduan refuses, flees, and is killed.

5.8–11 (July-Aug 54): The fleet lands in Britain and again a storm wrecks the ships. They are rebuilt and the Romans fortify a camp.

5.12–14 (July-Aug 54): Caesar provides a brief ethnography of the Britons.

5.15–22 (Aug-Sep 54): Caesar leads the Romans across the Thames into the territories of the British king Cassivellaunus, who launches sporadic attacks against the incoming armies. Caesar locates and seizes the stronghold of Cassivellaunus, who then fails to storm the Roman camp; he surrenders.

5.23–25 (Sep–Oct 54): The Romans return to Gaul. Caesar explains that due to a poor harvest the previous year, he is required to divide up his legions into more scattered winter camps than usual.

5.26–31 (Nov 54): The legates Sabinus and Cotta command a winter camp of fifteen cohorts among the Eburones. Ambiorix, their king, gives them warning of a coming pan-Gallic attack. In a debate, Sabinus suggests they evacuate the camp before the attack arrives, while Cotta advises that they remain and wait for Caesar's commands. Sabinus prevails, and the army leaves the camp at dawn.

5.32–39 (Nov 54): The departing Romans are ambushed by Ambiorix and are destroyed, despite their pleas for mercy. Emboldened by this success, the Nervii join the Eburones and they attack the legate Q. Cicero's camp of one legion in their territory.

5.40–48 (Nov 54): Q. Cicero rejects the Gauls' invitations to negotiate; in response, they surround the Roman camp and set it on fire. Refusing to submit, the Romans' numbers dwindle until word of the attack finally reaches Caesar, who quickly sends reinforcements.

5.49–53 (Dec 54): The Gauls move to face the approaching reinforcements. The Romans pretend to be afraid and unprepared; the Gauls fall for the trap and are chased away. Caesar joins Cicero and offers praise for his level-headed conduct. Word of this victory spreads, delighting the Romans and discouraging the Gauls.

5.54–58 (Winter 54–53): Hearing word of rebellions, Caesar subdues the Gauls with threats and entreaties. Indutiomarus of the Treveri gathers troops and attacks the legate Labienus, who feigns fear until his cavalry is dispatched. Indutiomarus is killed and peace returns to Gaul.

BOOK VI

6.1–8 (Mar–June 53): Continued signs of trouble in Gaul and from beyond the Rhine compel Caesar to launch a campaign early in the year. He begins with the Nervii, quickly subdues them, and calls all the leaders of Gaul to him. Those that do not show up are assumed to be hostile. The Gallic chief Acco begins an uprising among the Senones. Caesar plans to isolate Ambiorix by denying him support from other Gallic tribes, and defeats the Senones, Carnutes, and Menapii in swift succession. The Romans ravage the territory of the Menapii. The Treveri are then subdued.

6.9–10 (July–Aug 53): Caesar bridges the Rhine for a second time and discovers that the Suebi have mobilized, but will not face the Romans in battle.

6.11–28 (Summer 53): Caesar provides a lengthy ethnographic description of the Gauls and Germans.

6.30–34 (Sep 53): Caesar returns to Gaul, destroys the bridge, and attempts to apprehend Ambiorix in the Ardennes with cavalry. Ambiorix eludes capture and instructs the Eburones to scatter and hide. Caesar splits the legions into three forces and leaves their baggage train with the legate Q. Cicero at Atuatuca, an *oppidum* of the Eburones. The legions devastate the lands of the absent Eburones and invite the neighboring Gallic tribes to do likewise.

6.35–42 (Sep–Oct 53): The Germanic Sugambri cross the Rhine to join in the plunder, but are enticed by the prospect of looting the Roman baggage stored at Q. Cicero's camp. Unaware, Cicero sends out foraging parties which are ambushed, resulting in many casualties. Despite this, the camp manages to fend off the attack and the Sugambri return to Germania empty-handed. Caesar returns to the camp and criticizes Q. Cicero for not following his instructions.

6.43–44 (Oct–Dec 53): Frustrated by his inability to apprehend Ambiorix, Caesar orders the legions to continue their campaign of scorched earth. At the close of the year he returns to Durocortum, an *oppidum* of the Remi, and orders Acco to be executed. He then sends the legions into their winter camps and returns to Cisalpine Gaul.

The major tribes and towns of Gaul in the mid-1st century BCE

ABBREVIATIONS

abl: ablative

abs.: absolute

acc: accusative

BG: *dē bellō Gallicō*

BC: *bellum cīvile*

Caes.: Caesar

cl.: clause

dat: dative

e.g.: for example

fut.: future

gen: genitive

impers.: impersonal

impf.: imperfect

ind.: indirect

infin.: infinitive

lit.: literally

nom: nominative

part.: participle

pass.: passive

perf.: perfect

pl.: plural

PPP: perf. pass. part.

prep: preposition

pres.: present

rel.: relative

sc.: supply

sing.: singular

st.: statement

Verc.: Vercingetorix

A V A R I C V M

dē bellō Gallicō VII 1–28

with Running Vocabulary and Commentary

[1] *The Gauls plan a new uprising*

1 Quiētā Galliā Caesar, ut cōnstituerat, in Ītaliam ad conventūs agendōs proficīscitur. Ibi cognōscit dē Clōdiī caede senātūsque cōnsultō certior factus, ut omnēs iūniōrēs Ītaliae coniūrārent, dēlēctum tōtā prōvinciā habēre īnstituit.
2 Eae rēs in Galliam Trānsalpīnam celeriter perferuntur. Addunt ipsī et adfingunt rūmōribus Gallī, quod rēs poscere vidēbātur,

---

addō, -ere, -idī, -itus: add, insert, attach to, say in addition; increase
adfingō, -ere, -īnxī, -ictus: embellish; add to, attach; aggravate
caedis, -is f.: murder, assassination
cōnsultum, -ī n.: decision, resolution, plan; decree
conventus, -ūs m.: meeting, congregation, judicial assembly
dēlēctus, -ūs m.: levy, draft, conscription
īnstituō, -ere, -ī, -ūtus: establish; begin; determine, decide, resolve
poscō, -ere, poposcī, —: ask, demand
quiētus, a, um: inactive, calm

Galliā: for a brief introduction of the situation, see Introduction; for "Gauls" and other proper names in the text, see Appendix B
ut cōnstituerat: *as he had decided, determined*
in Ītaliam ad conventūs: Cisalpine Gaul. Roman provincial governors held judicial assemblies in their territories
senātūsque cōnsultō...coniūrārent: *and became better informed about the Senate's decree that all the young men of military age in Italy take the oath for military service*; this was a cautionary move by the Senate, and Caesar obeys the directive in the Italian (Cisalpine) portion of his province
quod rēs poscere vidēbātur: *which the situation seemed to demand/make inevitable*

retinērī urbānō mōtū Caesarem neque in tantīs dissēnsiōnibus ad exercitum venīre posse. 3 Hāc impulsī occāsiōne, quī iam ante sē populī Rōmānī imperiō subiectōs dolērent līberius atque audācius dē bellō cōnsilia inīre incipiunt. 4 Indictīs inter sē principēs Galliae conciliīs silvestribus ac remōtīs locīs queruntur dē Accōnis morte;

---

audācter: boldly, audaciously, confidently, fearlessly; impudently
concilium, -ī n.: public gathering, meeting; popular assembly, council
dissēnsiō, -ōnis f.: disagreement, quarrel; dissension, conflict
impellō, -ere, impulī, impulsus: drive, impel; urge on, incite
indicō (1): declare publicly; proclaim, announce; appoint
inēo, inīre, iniī, initus: enter; enter into; begin
līber, lībera, līberum: free, unrestricted
mors, mortis f.: death
occāsiō, -ōnis f.: opportunity; chance; pretext, occasion
queror, querī, questus: complain; protest, grumble, gripe
remōtus, -a, -um: remote; distant, far off; removed, withdrawn
retineō, -ēre, -uī, retentus: hold back, restrain; uphold; delay
silvestris, -e: wooded
subiciō, -ere, subiēcī, subiectus: throw under, place under; subdue; subject, submit

---

retinērī, posse: infinitive main verbs in ind. statement with subject *Caesarem*
urbānō mōtū: *by the urban commotion*; i.e. the unrest in the Roman capital
impulsī: *having been impelled*; PPP modifying *quī*
subiectōs: sc. *esse*; main verb of indirect statement introduced by *dolerent*
dē Accōnis morte: Acco had instigated a rebellion against Caesar among the Senones (*BG* 6.4.1), and was later harshly punished by Caesar: he was stripped, flogged to death, and then the corpse's head was removed (*BG* 6.44.2)

5 posse hunc cāsum ad ipsōs recidere dēmōnstrant; miserantur commūnem Galliae fortūnam; omnibus pollicitātiōnibus ac praemiīs dēposcunt quī bellī initium faciant et suī capitis perīculō Galliam in lībertātem vindicent.
6 In prīmīs ratiōnem esse habendam dīcunt, priusquam eōrum clandēstīna cōnsilia efferantur, ut Caesar ab exercitū interclūdātur.

---

cāsus, -ūs m.: incident; misfortune, calamity, plight
clandēstīnus, -a, -um: secret, hidden, concealed, clandestine
commūnis, -e: common, joint, public; general, universal
dēposcō, -scere, -poscī, —: demand; ask for earnestly; require
efferō, efferre, extulī, ēlātus: carry out; bring out; carry out for burial
interclūdō, -ere, -ūsī, -ūsus: cut off; blockade; hinder, block up
miseror, -ārī, -ātus: pity, feel sorry for; lament, bemoan
pollicitātiō, -ōnis f.: promise
priusquam: before; until; sooner than
recidō, -ere, -ī, recāsus: fall back, relapse, revert; fall upon, happen to

---

quī: relative clause of characteristic; they seek a tribe who have the right mindset to instigate the rebellion
in lībertātem vindicent: *set free* (idiom)
capitis perīculō: *from danger to their lives* (idiom)
in prīmīs ratiōnem...dīcunt: *they say that first of all, [the following] plan...*; the *ratiō* is specified by the upcoming *ut* clause

Id esse facile, 7 quod neque legiōnēs audeant absente imperātōre ex hībernīs ēgredī, neque imperātor sine praesidiō ad legiōnēs pervenīre possit. 8 Postrēmō in aciē praestāre interficī quam nōn veterem bellī glōriam lībertātemque quam ā maiōribus accēperint recuperāre.

---

audeō, -ēre, ausī, ausus: dare, act boldly, venture, risk
hīberna, -ōrum n.pl.: winter camp, winter quarters
interficiō, -ere, -fēcī, -fectus: kill; destroy
maiōrēs, -um m. pl.: ancestors
postrēmō: at last, finally
praestō (1): excel, surpass, be preferable to
recuperō (1): regain, restore, restore to health; refresh, recuperate

---

Id esse facile: infin. in indirect statement continuing from the previous sentence
audeant...possit: *will not dare...will not be able*; verbs in subordinate clauses within indirect statement are typically subjunctive
praestāre, interficī, recuperāre: *[they say that] it is preferable*; *praestāre* continues the ind. statement; *interficī* and *recuperāre* are compl. infinitives with *praestare*
lībertātem: The Gauls in *BG* consistently invoke the concept, both from the domination of each other (*BG* 1.17.3-4) and in the face of servitude to the Romans (*in eā lībertāte quam ā maiōribus accēperint permanēre quam Rōmānōrum servitūtem perferre mālint*, *BG* 3.8.4). Caesar suggests that all Gauls yearn for freedom inherently and are therefore easily incited to rebellion (*BG* 3.10.3). He further sees *lībertās* as the absence of *officium* and *disciplīna* (*BG* 4.1.9, in ref. to the Germans). Here, Verc. reiterates that *lībertās* is an ancient privilege common to all Gauls (cf. *BG* 5.27.6; 7.4.4 below; 7.37.2-4; 7.64.3; 7.71.3) and a prime motivator in their past and present uprisings (*BG* 7.76.2; 7.89.1-2; cf. 7.77.9-16). See Robin Seager in *Caesar against Liberty?*, ed. Cairns and Fantham (2003), 22-26
quam: *rather than*, with the implicit comparison of *praestāre*; the second *quam* is relative pronoun

[2] *The Carnutes offer to begin the war, and ask for pledges*

1 Hīs rēbus agitātīs profitentur Carnūtēs sē nūllum perīculum
commūnis salūtis causā recūsāre principēsque ex omnibus
bellum factūrōs pollicentur et, 2 quoniam in praesentiā
obsidibus cavēre inter sē nōn possint nē rēs efferātur, ut
iūreiūrandō ac fidē sanciātur petunt, collātīs mīlitāribus signīs
(quō mōre eōrum gravissima caerimōnia continētur), nē
factō initiō bellī ab reliquīs dēserantur.

---

agitō (1): drive; set in motion
caerimōnia, -ae f.: sacred rite
caveō, -ēre, -ī, cautus: avoid; take precautions
contineō, -ēre, -uī, -entus: hold together; secure
dēserō, -ere, -uī, -tus: desert
fidēs, -eī f.: faith
gravis, -e: heavy; serious; severe
iūsiūrandum, -ī n.: oath
mīlitāris, -e: of the military
mōs, mōris m.: habit, custom
polliceor, -ērī, -itus: promise
praesentia, -ae f.: present (time)
profiteor, -ērī, -fessus: declare
recūsō (1): refuse, reject
sanciō, -īre, sānxī, -ctus: make sacred; confirm

1-2: see Appendix A for a basic diagram of this sentence
causā: *for the sake of*
factūrōs: sc. *esse*
obsidibus: ablative of means
ut...sanciātur: *that it be solemnly assured by oath-swearing and trust*; this *ut*, with the subjunctive verb *sanciātur*, introduces an indirect command that functions as the object of main verb *petunt*
petunt: main verb introducing indirect command; subject is the Carnutes
nē...dēserantur: this noun clause serves as the subject of passive verb *sanciātur*, and explains the contents of the Gauls' oath

3 Tum, collaudātīs Carnūtibus, datō iūreiūrandō ab omnibus quī aderant, tempore eius reī cōnstitūtō ab conciliō discēditur.

---

adsum, -esse, adfuī, -futūrus: be in attendance
collaudō (1): commend
concilium, -ī n.: council
cōnstituō, -ere, -uī, -ūtus: set, station; draw up; halt; decide
iūsiūrandum, -ī n.: oath

---

tempore eius reī cōnstitūtō: *with the time of their deed being arranged*; abl. abs.
cōnstitūtō: the basic meaning of this verb is to place or establish, to halt, or to build something; in Caesar, it very often means to decide or resolve, except in the context of armies, when it usually means "draw up, muster, put in place"
ab conciliō: In addition to the fact that the Carnutes were the instigators of this most recent initiative, the territory of the Carnutes was a natural place for meetings between the various Gallic tribes, given the central location (see Introduction map). Caesar says that all the druids of Gaul assemble at a sacred place in the territory of the Carnutes (*in locō cōnsecrātō*, *BG* 6.13.10). Though he does not mention druids here, or in fact anywhere in *BG* VII, we can probably assume that these enigmatic priest-politicians were present at these important discussions. The Gauls in general seemed to have met *in conciliō* frequently, regardless of the tribes' varying political arrangements. For instance, in 58 BCE the assembled *principēs* of the Gauls had shown deference to Caesar (after the recent victory over the Helvetii) by asking his permission to have their council (*BG* 1.30-31). For war councils similar to the one here, see e.g. *BG* 2.10.4 and 3.18.3-6
discēditur: *they depart*; lit. "it is departed" (impers. pass.)

[3] *The Carnutes kill the Roman traders at Cenabum*

1 Ubi ea diēs vēnit, Carnūtēs Cotuātō et Conconnetodumnō ducibus, dēspērātīs hominibus, Cenabum signō datō concurrunt cīvēsque Rōmānōs, quī negōtiandī causā ibi cōnstiterant, in hīs Gāium Fūfium Citam, honestum equitem Rōmānum, quī reī frūmentāriae iussū Caesaris praeerat, interficiunt bonaque eōrum dīripiunt.

---

concurrō, -ere, -ī, -sus: assemble together; make haste; engage

cōnsisto, -ere, -stitī, -stitus: stop; settle

dīripio, -ere, -uī, direptus: plunder

negōtior, -ārī, -ātus: engage in business

praesum, -esse, -fuī, -futūrus: be in charge (of)

Cenabum: a town (*oppidum*) of the Carnutes, modern Orléans; it was a prosperous grain emporium controlling a key bridge over the Loire river

Cotuātō et Conconnetodumnō ducibus, dēspērātīs hominibus: *with nothing to lose, without hope,* or perhaps *reckless*; Caesar lists these two leaders the same way Romans would list the consuls of a given year. This same Cotuātus is mentioned again in *BG* book VIII under the alternate spelling "Gutuater"

negōtiandī: Roman citizens could be found well beyond the borders of the provinces; these were likely engaged in all manner of business, such as banking, money-lending, procuring slaves and supplies, arranging mining ventures, etc.

in hīs: *among whom*

reī frūmentāriae: *the grain supply*; dative indirect object of *praeerat*

bona…dīripiunt: *plundered their (the Romans') possessions*; the subject is the Carnutes

2 Celeriter ad omnēs Galliae cīvitātēs fāma perfertur. Nam ubicumque maior atque illūstrior incidit rēs, clāmōre per agrōs regiōnēsque significant; hunc aliī deinceps excipiunt et proximīs trādunt, ut tum accidit. 3 Nam quae Cenabī oriente sōle gesta essent, ante prīmam cōnfectam vigiliam in fīnibus Arvernōrum audīta sunt, quod spatium est mīlium passuum circiter centum LX.

---

accidō, -ere, -ī: occur; be heard
clāmor, -is m.: shout
cōnficiō, -ere, -fēcī, -fectus: make; prepare; complete
deinceps: in order; successively
excipiō, -ere, -cēpī, -ceptus: take up, receive; exempt; succeed
illūstris, -tre: noteworthy; clear, prominent; famous; bright
incidō, -ere, -ī, —: happen, visit
perferō, -ferre, -tulī, -lātus: carry through; announce
proximus, -a, -um.: nearest; adjoining
significō (1): show, indicate
sōl, sōlis m.: the sun
ubicumque: wherever, in whatever place; in any place
vigilia, -ae f.: one shift of guard duty in the Roman system; there were four *vigiliae* per night

---

significant: the subject is the Gauls
ut tum accidit: *as happened at this time*
quae…gesta essent: *for although the deeds had been done at Cenabum at dawn;* indirect question – the *quae* here is equivalent to the adversative phrase *cum ea*, and has thus adopted an adversative force
oriente sōle: ablative of time when, with pres. part. from *orior*
mīlium passuum circiter centum LX: *about one hundred and sixty miles*; literally "a hundred and sixty thousands of paces," a Roman mile being (roughly) one thousand soldier's paces (including a step with left and right foot) or about 1480m

[4] *The entrance of Vercingetorix*

1 Similī ratiōne ibi Vercingetorīx, Celtillī fīlius, Arvernus, summae potentiae adulēscēns, cuius pater principātum Galliae tōtīus obtinuerat et ob eam causam, quod rēgnum appetēbat, ab cīvitāte erat interfectus, convocātīs suīs clientibus facile incendit.

---

adulēscēns, -centis m./f.: a youth
appetō, -ere, -īvī, -ītus: seek, desire; long for
cōnvocō (1): assemble, summon
incendō, -ere, -dī, -census: set fire to, inflame; rouse, incite
obtineō, -ēre, -uī, -tentus: get hold of; maintain; obtain
potentia, -ae f.: power; ability; virtue
principātus, -ūs m.: rule, dominion
rēgnum, -ī n.: kingship, rule; domain, a kingdom

---

similī ratiōne: *in like manner*; that is, Verc. attempts a similar agitation of the Arverni as had occurred among the Carnutes
summae potentiae: genitive of description; *potentia* can mean physical might, ability, or even virtue
clientibus: in Roman terms, *clientēs* were those in a position of obligation to a more powerful *patrōnus*; here and elsewhere Caesar employs the Roman concept to describe similar relationships among the Gauls. The Gallic *clientes*, as labeled by Caesar, were of lower status than other dependent members of Gallic society like *ambactī* (see *BG* 6.15.2) or *soldūriī* (*BG* 3.2.12)
incendit: Caesar's word choice here is noteworthy, as *incendit* translates literally as "set on fire," showing Verc.'s extraordinary ability to excite the crowds

2 Cōgnitō eius cōnsiliō ad arma concurritur. Prohibētur ab Gobannitiōne, patruō suō, reliquīsque principibus, quī hanc temptandam fortūnam nōn exīstimābant; expellitur ex oppidō Gergoviā; 3 nōn dēstitit tamen atque in agrīs habet dīlēctum egentium ac perditōrum. Hāc coāctā manū, quōscumque adit ex cīvitāte ad suam sententiam perdūcit;

---

concurrō, -ere, -ī, -sus: assemble together; make haste; engage

dēsistō, -ere, -stitī, -stitus: stop, cease, desist, leave off

dīlēctus, -ūs m.: draft, conscription, recruitment

egēns, egentis: poor, destitute

perditus, -a, -um: lost, desperate; corrupt, incorrigible

perdūcō, -ere, -ūxī, -uctus: lead, guide; prolong; induce, conduct

quī-, quae-, quodcumque: whoever, whatever

temptō (1): test, try

Gobannitiōne, patruō suō: Verc.'s uncle

principibus: the most important individuals of the tribe or town

hanc temptandam fortūnam: *that this outcome must be attempted*

nōn dēstitit tamen: *nevertheless, he did not desist; tamen* is post-positive

in agrīs habet dīlēctum egentium ac perditōrum: Verc. is rejected by the elites in the urban areas, but finds support among the peasants in rural areas and those who are presumably fed up with the leadership

Hāc coactā manū: *once he had gathered this band;* in military contexts, *manus* often translates as "[armed] group" or "band"

4 hortātur ut commūnis lībertātis causā arma capiant, magnīsque coāctīs cōpiīs adversāriōs suōs, ā quibus paulō ante erat ēiectus, expellit ex cīvitāte. 5 Rēx ab suīs appellātur. Dīmittit quōque versus lēgātiōnēs; obtestātur ut in fide maneant.

---

appello (1): label as, apply to; call upon; address
communis, -e: common, joint, public; general, universal
dīmittō, -ere, -mīsī, -missus: send forth, distribute; scatter
ēiciō, -ere, -iēcī, -iectus: cast out, expel, discharge, exile
expellō, -ere, -pulī, -pulsus: drive out, expel, banish
obtestor, -āri, -ātus: call as witness, swear; entreat, implore
quis-, quae-, quodque: each
versus: toward, in the direction of

ā quibus paulō ante: *by whom, a little while before*
Rēx ab suīs appellātur: Verc. has essentially engineered a rural popular uprising against the status quo leadership of the Arverni, promising "freedom for all Gauls." Such intra-tribal factional maneuvering is not uncommon (cf. *BG* 1.3-4, e.g.). The title of *rēx* is significant, as Verc.'s father had been executed by the Arverni for seeking that distinction (7.4.1). The Arverni were a powerful force in Gallic politics and enjoyed a long history of dominating other tribes (see Appendix B). In the coming conflict there will be a certain tension among the Gauls between suspicion of the hegemony of one tribe or leader and pursuit of freedom from Roman domination (see note on *lībertās* 7.1.8 above)
quōque versus: *towards each direction*, i.e. "in every direction;" *versus* is an adverb which tends to follow the word it modifies, and *quōque* here is not the adverb, but from *quisque* "each" (*quōque* [*locō*])

6 Celeriter sibi Sēnōnēs, Parīsiōs, Pictonēs, Cadurcōs, Turonōs, Aulercōs, Lemovīcēs, Andōs reliquōsque omnēs quī Ōceanum attingunt adiungit: omnium cōnsēnsū ad eum dēfertur imperium. 7 Quā oblātā potestāte omnibus hīs cīvitātibus obsidēs imperāt, certum numerum mīlitum ad sē celeriter addūcī iubet; 8 armōrum quantum quaeque cīvitās domī quodque ante tempus efficiat cōnstituit; in prīmīs equitātuī studet.

---

adiungō, -ere, -xī, -ctus: add, attach, support; apply to; harness
attingō, -ere, -ī, attāctus: touch, touch/border on; reach, arrive at
cōnsēnsus, -ūs m.: agreement, concord; plot, conspiracy
dēferō, -ferre, -tulī, -lātus: grant, confer; carry off, convey
offerō, -ferre, -tulī, -lātus: show, present; cause; confer; inflict
studeō, -ēre, -uī, —: (+ dat) be eager for, apply effort to

---

reliquōsque omnēs: there is an implied "tribes" here
Quā oblātā potestāte omnibus: ablative absolute
quodque ante tempus: *and before what time*
Sēnōnēs...Andōs: all of these peoples were north and west of the Arverni except the Cardurcī, who were to the south and west. Except for the Senones (see Appendix B), these were all relatively small tribes. See Introduction map
obsidēs: a common method for ensuring compliance in agreements was the exchange of hostages, among both Gauls and Romans; Caesar had also taken hostages numerous times while fighting in Gaul and Britain; see Moscovich, "*Obsidibus Traditis*: Hostages in Caesar's *De Bello Gallico*," *Classical Journal* 75.2 (1979): 122-28
in prīmīs equitātuī studet: *in particular he is interested in cavalry*. Verc.'s strategy will focus on his forces being more mobile than Roman legions

9 Summae dīligentiae summam imperī sevēritātem addit; magnitūdine supplicī dubitantēs cōgit. 10 Nam maiōre commissō dēlīctō igne atque omnibus tormentīs necat, leviōre dē causā auribus dēsectīs aut singulīs effossīs oculīs domum remittit, ut sint reliquīs documentō et magnitūdine poenae perterreant aliōs.

---

addō, -ere, -didī, -itus: place upon; attach; increase, join
auris, -is f.: ear
dēlīctum, -ī n.: fault, offense
dēsecō, -āre, -cuī, -ctus: sever; cut off (as a limb)
documentum, -ī n.: lesson, warning, example
dubitō (1): hesitate, waver; delay
effodiō, -ere, -ī, -fossus: dig out, excavate; gouge out
levis, -e: light, slight; trivial, petty
magnitūdō, -inis f.: size; extent
necō, -āre, -uī, -ctus: kill, murder
oculus, -ī m.: eye
poena, -ae f.: punishment
supplicium, -ī n.: punishment, suffering; torture

---

dīligentiae...severitātem: Verc. exhibits two of the virtues typical of a Roman aristocrat; others included *honestās, gravitās, dignitās, auctōritās, pietās,* and *vēritās*
igne atque omnibus tormentīs necat: *he killed with fire and all kinds of tortures*
auribus dēsectīs aut singulīs effossīs oculīs: abl. abs.; we cannot know the truth of Caesar's claims here, but it is certainly the case that Verc. was able to compel the Gauls more effectively than anyone else in the previous seven years of war
ut sint reliquīs documentō: *that they might be a warning for the others;* a double dative construction

[5] *The Bituriges and the Aedui consider their options*

1 Hīs suppliciīs celeriter coāctō exercitū Luctērium
Cadurcum, summae hominem audāciae, cum parte cōpiārum
in Rutēnōs mittit; ipse in Biturigēs proficīscitur. Eius adventū
Biturigēs ad Aeduōs, 2 quōrum erant in fide, lēgātōs mittunt
subsidium rogātum, quō facilius hostium cōpiās sustinēre
possint.

---

audācia, -ae f.: boldness, courage, confidence; recklessness, audacity
fidēs, -eī f.: trust, faith, confidence
proficīscor, -ficīscī, -fectus: depart, set out; proceed
rogō (1): ask, invite; introduce
subsidium, -iī n.: help, relief; reinforcement
supplicium, -iī n.: punishment; petition
sustineō, -ēre, -uī, -entus: (here) bear; endure; hold back (elsewhere) support; nourish

---

coāctō exercitū: *with the army having been collected;* ablative absolute; *suppliciīs* is abl. of means
Lucterius: a leader among the Cadurcī and a lieutenant of Verc.; his role in Caesar's account here is minimal, but he would play a major role in the fighting of the following year, as described in *BG* VIII
summae hominem audāciae: *person of greatest boldness;* the hyperbaton of *hominem* here emphasizes this quality of Lucterius
ipse: Vercingetorix
Aeduōs: for the Aedui, see Appendix B
rogātum: *to ask for, to seek*; a supine
quō...possint: *by which (subsidium) they might be able to endure/hold back the forces of the enemy more easily*; a rel. clause of purpose

3 Aeduī dē cōnsiliō lēgātōrum, quōs Caesar ad exercitum relīquerat, cōpiās equitātūs peditātūsque subsidiō Biturigibus mittunt. 4 Quī cum ad flūmen Ligerim vēnissent quod Biturigēs ab Aeduīs dīvidit, paucōs diēs ibi morātī neque flūmen trānsīre 5 ausī domum revertuntur lēgātīsque nostrīs renūntiant sē Biturigum perfidiam veritōs revertisse,

---

audeō, -ēre, -sus: dare, venture, risk
dīvidō, -ere, -vīsi, -vīsus: divide, separate; share, distribute; distinguish
moror, -ārī, -ātus: delay
perfidia, -ae f.: faithlessness, treachery
renūntiō (1): report, announce; reject
revertor, -tī, -sus: turn back, go back, return; recur
subsidium, -iī n.: help; reserve of soldiers
vereor, -ērī, -itus: to fear, revere, respect

---

lēgātōrum: these are Roman military advisers which Caesar had left with the Aedui; not to be confused with the messengers sent by the Gauls above, or with Caesar's direct lieutenants (like Labienus), who are also called *lēgātī*
subsidiō Biturigibus: *as a source of aid for the Bituriges*; double dative constr.
flūmen Ligerim: the modern Loire. See Appendix B
sē Birturigum perfidiam veritōs revertisse: *that they [themselves] returned having feared treachery of the Bituriges;* ind. statement with *perfidiam* as the direct object and *veritōs* as a deponent perfect passive participle modifying *sē*

quibus id consilī fuisse cognōverint ut, sī flūmen trānsīssent, ūnā ex parte ipsī, alterā Arvernī sē circumsisterent. 6 Id eāne dē causā quam lēgātīs prōnūntiārunt, an perfidiā adductī fēcerint, quod nihil nōbīs cōnstat, nōn vidētur prō certō esse prōpōnendum. 7 Biturigēs eōrum discessū statim cum Arvernīs iunguntur.

---

circumsistō, -ere, -tetī, —: stand, gather, crowd; surround,
cōnstō, -āre, -itī, —: is certain, fixed, agreed upon
iungō, -ere, -ūnxī, -ūnctus: join, unite; bring together, harness
nihil: (as noun) nothing; (as adverb) not at all, in no way
perfidia, -ae f.: treachery
prōnūntiō (1): announce; proclaim; relate
prōpōnō, -ere, -suī, -situs: display; proclaim; propose; relate

---

quibus id consilī fuisse cognōverint: *for whom they had ascertained there to be the following plan*
trānsīssent: the Aedui forces, that is, and **ipsī** being the Bituriges
Id eāne dē causā...an: *whether...or*; the *-ne* indicates a double question, and the second question is introduced by *an*
quod...prōpōnendum: *because it is in no way certain to me, it does not seem proper that [this opinion] be put forth as a certainty; nihil* is adverbial, and *vidētur* is used not only in its passive mode as "it seems," but also the more rare "it seems proper" or "is seemly." See Appendix A for a basic diagram. Caes. does not trust the Aedui's account of these events, and what he writes here is nearly a *praeteritiō*. He will continue in this mistrust as he attempts to rejoin his legions via Aedui territory. The Aedui had been loyal "friends and allies" of the Romans in Gaul for years, but Caesar's doubt of them here will prove to be warranted in the coming weeks (see *BG* VII 32-43)

[6] *Caesar ponders how to reach his forces*

1 Hīs rēbus in Ītaliam Caesarī nūntiātīs, cum iam ille urbānās rēs virtūte Cn. Pompēī commodiōrem in statum pervēnisse intellegeret, in Trānsalpīnam Galliam profectus est. 2 Eō cum vēnisset, magnā difficultāte adficiēbātur quā ratiōne ad exercitum pervenīre posset. 3 Nam sī legiōnēs in prōvinciam arcesseret, sē absente in itinere proeliō dīmicātūrās intellegēbat; 4 sī ipse ad exercitum contenderet, nē eīs quidem eō tempore quī quiētī vidērentur suam salūtem rēctē committī vidēbat.

---

adficiō, -ere, adfēcī, adfectus: affect; move, influence; afflict
arcessō, -ere, -īvī, -ītus: send for, summon, invite; fetch
commodus, -a, -um: suitable, convenient, obliging; favorable
contendō, -ere, -dī, -tus: strain; hurry
dīmicō (1): struggle, be in peril
eō: to/toward that place
quiēscō, -ere, -ēvī, -ētus: rest, be at peace, be still/inactive
rēctē: rightly, correctly, properly
status, -ūs m.: position, situation, condition; rank; standing

---

urbānās rēs: i.e., the tumultuous events of the recent past back in Rome
quā ratiōne...posset: *as to the means by which he might be able to reach his army*; indirect question; the legions were scattered around Gaul in their winter camps
sē absente: ablative absolute; *sē* is ablative singular referring to Caesar
dīmicātūrās: *[the legions] would be in peril*; future infinitive; Caesar had regularly trusted his *lēgātī* to lead the legions independently in the past, but now inexplicably considers the soldiers helpless without him. It would seem more prudent to call them south rather than travel alone in secret to join them
nē eīs quidem...quī: *not even to those [Gauls] who*

[7] *Caesar organizes a defense of the province*

1 Interim Luctērius Cadurcus in Rutēnōs missus eam cīvitātem Arvernīs conciliat. 2 Prōgressus in Nitiobrīgēs et Gabalōs ab utrīsque obsidēs accipit et magnā coāctā manū in prōvinciam Narbōnem versus ēruptiōnem facere contendit.

---

conciliō (1): win over, procure; reconcile; commend
contendō, -ere, -dī, -tus: strain; hurry
ēruptiō, -iōnis f.: sudden rush of troops from a position; a sortie
manus, -ūs m.: hand; (here) band, group
prōgredior, -ī, -gressus: go/march forward, march forward
uter-, utra-, utrumque: each (of two)
versus: toward, in the direction of

Rutēnōs: a small tribe directly south of the Arverni and traditionally subject to them. Their *oppidum* was Segodunum, modern Rodez. The southern part of their territory had been seized by the Romans after the defeat of the Arverni coalition in 121 BCE; Caesar calls the tribesmen of this southern portion *Rutēnī prōvinciālēs* (see 7.7.4 below)
missus: *having been dispatched;* perfect passive participle
Arvernīs: dative with *conciliat* "win over to/for, acquire for"
Nitiobrīgēs et Gabalōs: two small tribes on the southwestern and southern borders of the Arverni, respectively
magnā coāctū manū: *with a large band having been collected;* in military contexts, *manus* often translates as "[armed] group" or "band"
Narbōnem: modern Narbonne, a major Roman port city in Transalpine Gaul ("the Province") situated on the Via Domitia and Via Aquitania between Spain and Italy

3 Quā rē nūntiātā Caesar omnibus cōnsiliīs antevertendum existimāvit ut Narbōnem proficīscerētur. 4 Eō cum vēnisset, timentēs cōnfirmat, praesidia in Rutēnīs prōvinciālibus, Volcīs Arecomicīs, Tolōsātibus circumque Narbōnem, quae loca hostibus erant fīnitima, cōnstituit; 5 partem cōpiārum ex prōvinciā supplēmentumque, quod ex Ītaliā addūxerat, in Helviōs, quī fīnēs Arvernōrum contingunt, convenīre iubet.

---

antevertō, -ere, -ī, —: prefer, place before; precede; anticipate (+ dat)

cōnfirmō (1): secure; reassure

fīnitimus, -a, -um: neighboring, bordering, adjoining

locō (1): place, station; arrange; contract (for)

prōvinciālis, -e: pertaining to a province (here, to *Trānsalpīna*)

supplēmentum, -ī n.: supplies, reinforcements

---

antevertendum: sc. *esse*; passive periphrastic infinitive of an indirect statement introduced by *existimāvit*

ut Narbōnem proficīscerētur: substantive noun clause acting as the accusative singular subject of *antevertendum*

eō: *to that place*

Volcīs Arecomīcīs, Tolōsātibus: two small Gallic tribes living in the Roman province near Narbo; here, Caes. intends to protect Narbo and places garrisons in four strategic places

in: *among, within the borders of*; common shorthand in Caes.

Helviōs: see Appendix B

[8] *Caesar suddenly attacks the Arverni*

1 Hīs rēbus comparātīs, repressō iam Luctēriō et remōtō,
quod intrāre intrā praesidia perīculōsum putābat, in Helviōs
proficīscitur. 2 Etsī mōns Cevenna, quī Arvernōs ab Helviīs
disclūdit, dūrissimō tempore annī altissimā nive iter
impediēbat, tamen discussā nive sex in altitūdinem pedum

---

altus, -a, -um: high; deep
comparō (1): prepare; provide
disclūdō, -ere, -lūsī, -lūsus: divide, separate, keep apart
discutiō, -ere, -cussī, -cussus: shatter; dissipate, remove
dūrus, -a, -um: harsh, severe
impediō, -īre, -īvī, -ītus: hinder, hamper, obstruct
intrō (1): enter; go into, penetrate; reach
mōns, montis m.: mountain
nix, nivis f.: snow
removeō, -ēre, -ī, -tus: withdraw, move back, take away, set aside
reprimō, -ere, -pressī, -pressus: press back; check, prevent, restrain

---

comparātīs; repressō; remōtō: all three are abl. abs.
intrāre...perīculōsum: sc. *esse*; the infinitive is the subject of the indirect statement after *putābat*; note that Lucterius is the subject of *putābat*, not Caesar, though an understood *Caesar* is the subject of *proficīscitur*
mōns Cevenna: now called the Cevennes mountains, in southwestern France
discussā nīve: abl. abs.; Roman soldiers carried shovels as part of their kit, but presumably not snow shovels
sex in altitūdinem pedum: *to a depth of six feet; sex* modifies *pedum,* translate *in* as "to"

atque ita viīs patefactīs summō mīlitum sūdōre ad fīnēs Arvernōrum pervēnit. 3 Quibus oppressīs inopīnantibus, quod sē Cevennā ut mūrō mūnītōs exīstimābant, ac nē singulārī quidem umquam hominī eō tempore annī sēmitae patuerant, equitibus imperat ut quam lātissimē possint vagentur et quam maximum hostibus terrōrem īnferant.

īnferō, -ferre, -tulī, -lātus: bring in, import; inflict; obtain
inopīnāns, -antis: unaware, off guard; unexpected
lātus, -a, -um: wide; extensive
mūnītus, -a, -um: defended, fortified; protected, secured, safe
opprimō, -ere, -pressī, -pressus: press down; suppress; overthrow
patefacio, -ere, -fēcī, -factus: open up; reveal, disclose, expose
patēo, -ēre, -uī, —: stand open, be open; extend
sēmita, -ae f.: path
sūdor, -is m.: sweat; hard labor
umquam: ever, at any time
vagor, -ārī, -ātus: wander, roam

Quibus oppressīs inopīnantibus: abl. abs; the Arverni are caught off-guard
sē Cevennā...mūnītōs exīstimābant: *they were thinking that they were protected by [Mount] Cevenna; mūnītōs* with an implied *esse* in ind. statement
ut murō: *as if by a wall;* not used here to introduce a result or purpose clause
nē singulārī quidem...hominī: *not even for lone individual [travelers]*
quam lātissimē possint: *as widely as possible;* lit. "as widely as they could"
quam maximum...terrōrem: *as much terror as possible;* superlative

4 Celeriter haec fāmā ac nūntiīs ad Vercingetorīgem perferuntur; quem perterritī omnēs Arvernī circumsistunt atque obsecrant ut suīs fortūnīs cōnsulat, nēve ab hostibus dīripiantur, praesertim cum videat omne ad sē bellum trānslātum. 5 Quōrum ille precibus permōtus castra ex Biturigibus movet in Arvernōs versus.

---

ad: about (with numerals)
circumsistō, -ere, -stetī,: stand, gather, crowd; surround, beset
cōnsulō, -ere, -uī, -tus: (+ acc): consult; (+ dat): consider, have a care for
dīripiō, -ere, -uī, -reptus: tear apart; lay waste, plunder, pillage
nūntius, -iī m.: messenger; report
obsecrō (1): entreat, beseech, implore, pray
perferō, -ferre, -tulī, -lātus: carry through; announce
permoveō, -ēre, -ī, -tus: move deeply; influence
praesertim: especially; particularly
prex, precis f.: prayer, request

---

quem: refers to Vercingetorix
perterritī: *having been thoroughly terrified;* PPP modifying *omnēs Arvernī*
ut suīs fortūnīs cōnsulat: indirect command
ad sē: *to their lands, onto their heads*
trānslatūm: sc. *esse;* from *trānsferre*
Quōrum...precibus permōtus: *deeply moved by their prayers*

[9] *Caesar goes to Vienna, then gathers his legions*

1 At Caesar bīduum in hīs locīs morātus, quod haec dē Vercingetorīge ūsū ventūra opīniōne praecēperat, per causam supplēmentī equitātūsque cōgendī ab exercitū discēdit; Brūtum adulēscentem hīs cōpiīs praeficit; 2 hunc monet ut in omnēs partēs equitēs quam lātissimē pervagentur; datūrum sē operam nē longius trīduō ab castrīs absit.

---

bīduum, bīduuī n.: two days
lātē: broadly, widely, extensively
moror, -ārī, -ātus: delay; remain
pervagor, -vagārī, -vagātus: wander, range about; spread out
praecipiō, -cipere, -cēpī, -ceptus: take in advance, anticipate
praeficiō, -ficere, -fēcī, -fectus: place in command (+ acc & dat)
trīduum, trīduī n.: three days

---

quod haec...praecēperat: a difficult section; *because he* [Caes.] *had anticipated by conjecture that these things would in fact come about regarding Verc.* (that is, that Verc. would move towards him); *ūsū venīre* is an idiom for "occur, actually happen, befall"

per causam: *on the pretext of*; this phrase is rare in Caes., appearing only here in *BG*. It appears in Caes. *BC* three times, e.g. at 3.24.1, when M. Antonius sends two ships out into the Brundisium harbor on the pretext of rowing practice (*per causam exercendōrum rēmigum*) in order to lure in Libo's blockading ships. Livy also uses *per causam* with this meaning, e.g. 2.32.1

cōgendī: *of gathering;* gerundive with the genitive nouns

Brutum: Decimus Iunius Brutus Albinus, not to be confused with Marcus Iunius, though Decimus would also be one of Caesar's assassins in 44. As Caesar's *lēgātus* he had defeated the Veneti in a sea battle in 56 and would again command a fleet in the siege of Massalia in 49 BCE during the Civil War

datūrum sē operam: [Caes. tells Brutus that] *he will make an effort that*

3 Hīs cōnstitūtīs rēbus, suīs inopīnantibus quam māximīs potest itineribus Viennam pervēnit. 4 Ibi nactus recentem equitātum, quem multīs ante diēbus eō praemīserat, neque diurnō neque nocturnō itinere intermissō per fīnēs Aeduōrum in Lingonēs contendit, ubi duae legiōnēs hiemābant, ut, sī quid etiam dē suā salūte ab Aeduīs inīrētur cōnsilī, celeritāte praecurreret.

---

contendō, -ere, -dī, -tus: strain; hurry
diurnus, -a, -um: daytime
fīnis, -is f.: boundary; (pl.) territory
hiemō (1): pass the winter
inopīnāns, inopīnantis: unaware; unexpecting, surprised
intermittō, -ere, -mīsī, -missus: leave off, omit; interrupt; let pass
iter, itineris n.: route, journey
nancīscor, -cīscī, nactus: obtain
nocturnus, -a, -um: nighttime
praecurrō, -ere, -cucurrī, — : run before; precede; anticipate
recēns, -entis: (here) fresh

---

suīs inopīnantibus: *his own [soldiers] being unaware*; abl. abs.; Caes. moved so quickly that not even his own forces realized what was happening
quam māximīs potest itineribus: *with greatest possible marches*; Caes. was known for rapid marches, but these efforts were apparently extraordinary even for him
Viennam: not the Austrian city, but an *oppidum* of the Allobroges 35km south of Lyon, at the confluence of the Gère and the Rhône. Under Augustus it would become *Colonia Julia Augusta Florentia Viennensium*, and today is known for its well-preserved Roman ruins
hiemābant: the legions spent the winter in fortified *castra* throughout Gaul
si quid...inīrētur cōnsiliī: *if any plan was being devised*; the Aedui had been solid allies of the Romans for years, but here Caes. reminds us just how powerful, and therefore dangerous, they could be. For their role in the present crisis, see *BG* 7.32-43

5 Eō cum pervēnisset, ad reliquās legiōnēs mittit priusque omnēs in ūnum locum cōgit quam dē eius adventū Arvernīs nūntiārī posset. 6 Hāc rē cognitā Vercingetorīx rūrsus in Biturigēs exercitum redūcit atque inde profectus Gorgobinam, Boiōrum oppidum, quōs ibi Helvēticō proeliō vīctōs Caesar collocāverat Aeduīsque attribuerat, oppūgnāre īnstituit.

---

attribuō, -ere, -buī, -būtus: assign, allot to; put under jurisdiction of (+ dat)
collocō (1): place, arrange; station
inde: from there; thereafter
īnstituō, -ere, -uī, -tūtus: prepare; draw up; build, construct
rūrsus: backward; on the contrary, in return; in turn, again

Eō: *to that place,* i.e. the *castra* among the Lingones
mittit: *sends word to*
reliquās legiōnēs: In the previous book (6.44.3), Caes. describes the distribution of his winter camps: six legions at Agendincum among the Senones, two legions to the east among the Lingones, and two legions to the north on the borders of the Treveri
prius...quam...posset: *earlier than it might be possible to be reported to the Arverni about his arrival*
Hāc rē cognitā: abl. abs.
Gorgobinam: the *oppidum* of a Boii enclave in the territory of the Aedui and subject to them. As he explains here, Caes. had "permitted" the Aedui to give the town to Boii refugees after the defeat of the Helvetii coalition in 58 (*BG* 1.28.5)

[10] *Caesar decides to help the Boii, despite supply problems*

1 Magnam haec rēs Caesarī difficultātem ad cōnsilium capiendum adferēbat: sī reliquam partem hiemis ūnō locō legiōnēs continēret, nē stīpendiāriīs Aeduōrum expugnātīs cūncta Gallia dēficeret, quod nūllum amīcīs in eō praesidium vidērētur positum esse; sī mātūrius ex hībernīs ēdūceret, nē ab rē frūmentāriā dūrīs subvectiōnibus labōrāret.

---

adferō, -ferre, -tulī, -lātus: convey; allege, announce; cause
contineō, -ēre, -uī, -tentus: secure, maintain, sustain
dēficiō, -ere, -fēcī, -fectus: (here) move away, withdraw, revolt
dūrus, -a, -um: harsh, severe
ēdūcō, -ere, -ūxī, -uctus: lead out; draw up; bring up
hīberna, -ōrum n.pl.: winter camp, winter quarters
hiems, -is f.: winter
mātūrus, -a, -um: early, speedy
stīpendiārius, -a, -um: tributary, liable to another; mercenary
subvectiō, -iōnis f.: transporting (of supplies) to a center

---

ad cōnsilium capiendum: *as far as making a plan*; this *ad* + gerundive does not have the typical translation "for the purpose of"
nē...nē: these both introduce fear clauses, introduced and implied by Caesar's *magna difficultās* in the first sentence; see Appendix A
stīpendiāriīs Aeduōrum expugnātīs: *with the tribes subordinate to the Aedui having been overcome*; abl. abs.
quod...vidērētur: *because it would appear that* + ind. statement
nūllum amīcīs in eō praesidium: *no protection for friends by him* (Caes.)
ab rē frūmentāriā: *in regards to the supply of provisions*; this usage of *ab* is common with *labōrāre, dolēre,* and *valēre*
dūrīs subvectiōnibus: ablative of cause, also frequent with *labōrāre*

2 Praestāre vīsum est tamen omnēs difficultātēs perpetī quam tantā contumēliā acceptā omnium suōrum voluntātēs aliēnāre. 3 Itaque cohortātus Aeduōs dē supportandō commeātū praemittit ad Boiōs quī dē suō adventū doceant hortenturque ut in fidē maneant atque hostium impetum magnō animō sustineant. 4 Duābus Agedincī legiōnibus atque impedīmentīs tōtīus exercitūs relictīs ad Boiōs proficīscitur.

---

aliēnō (1): alienate, give up, lose possession, estrange
commeātus, -ūs m.: supplies, food
contumēlia, -ae f.: indignity, affront, insult; assault, violence
perpetior, -petī, -pessus: endure to the full
praemittō, -ere, -mīsī, -missus: send ahead or forward
praestō (1): excel, surpass, be superior (to)
supportō (1): carry up, transport
sustineō, -ēre, -uī, -entus: support; check; put off
voluntās, -ātis f.: will, desire; purpose; good will

---

praestāre vīsum est tamen: *it seemed nevertheless better*
quam: *rather than;* with *praestāre*
praemittit...quī...doceant hortenturque: rel. clause of purpose after a verb of sending; there is an understood "messengers" with *praemittit* which is the antecedent of the *quī*
ut in fide maneant: (*urge*) *that they remain in good faith*; ind. command
Agedincī: the chief *oppidum* of the Senones, in the vicinity of modern Sens on the river Yonne. It was a convenient Roman base of operations because it was fortified, centrally located, and in the territory of a recently subdued tribe. Leaving two legions and the *impedimenta* here, Caes. will employ the remaining eight legions for the subsequent events of this volume, 40,000+ men

[11] *Caesar takes Vellaunodunum and Cenabum*

1 Alterō diē cum ad oppidum Sēnōnum Vellaunodūnum vēnisset, nē quem post sē hostem relinqueret, quō expedītiōre rē frūmentāriā ūterētur, oppugnāre īnstituit idque bīduō circumvāllāvit; 2 tertiō diē missīs ex oppidō lēgātīs dē dēditiōne arma cōnferrī, iūmenta prōdūcī, sēscentōs obsidēs darī iubet. 3 Ea quī cōnficeret Gāium Trebōnium lēgātum relinquit.

---

bīduum, -uī n.: two-day period
circumvāllō (1): surround with siegeworks; blockade
cōnferō, -ferre, -tulī, -lātus: bring together; gather; unite
cōnficiō, -ere, -fēcī, -fectus: make; prepare; complete
dēditiō, -is f.: surrender
expedītus, -a, -um: free, unencumbered; convenient
iūmentum, -ī n.: mule, horse, or other beast of burden
lēgātus, -ī m.: (in sentence 2) ambassador; (in sentence 3) lieutenant, legate
prōdūcō, -ere, -dūxī, -ductus: lead forward, bring out, reveal
sescentī, -ae, -a: 600
ūtor, ūtī, ūsus: use, employ; enjoy (+ abl)

Vellaunodūnum: a smaller *oppidum* of the Senones, otherwise unknown
quem: *aliquem* becomes *quem* after *nē*
quō: *so that*; the abl. *quō* (= *ut eō*) is freq. the subordinating conjunction in final purpose clauses containing a comp. adj.; see A&G §531a
bīduō: abl. of time within which
ea quī cōnficeret: *so that he might complete these arrangements*; rel. cl. of purpose after *relinquit*
Trebōnium: see Appendix B

Ipse, ut quam prīmum iter faceret, Cenabum Carnūtum proficīscitur; 4 quī tum prīmum allātō nūntiō dē oppugnātiōne Vellaunodūnī, cum longius eam rem ductum īrī exīstimārent, praesidium Cenabī tuendī causā quod eō mitterent comparābant. Hūc bīduō pervēnit.

---

afferō, -ferre, attulī, allātus: report, allege, announce
comparō (1): prepare; provide
hūc: to this place
nūntius, -iī m.: missive, messenger
tueor, tuērī, tūtus: to defend, guard
ūsus, -ūs m.: use, practice, exercise

---

ut...iter faceret: *in order that he make the journey*; purpose clause
quam primum: *as soon as possible*; *quam* + superlative
quī: he means the Carnutes
tum prīmum: *then for the first time; at that very moment*
cum: *because*; causal *cum* clause
ductum īrī: *would be drawn out*; a rare fut. pass. infin. in ind. statement
praesidium...quod eō mitterent: *a troop of reinforcements which they might send there*
tuendī causā: *for the sake of defending*; gerundive
Ipse...pervēnit: in this section Caes. is keen to emphasize the rapidity and decisiveness of his assault on Cenabum, where the killing of the Roman *negōtiātōrēs* had taken place back in 3.1. Note his use of temporal expressions here (*quam prīmum*; *tum prīmum*; *longius*; *bīduō*). The Carnutes suddenly found themselves under attack at two of their major *oppida* in succession; Vellaunodūnum capitulates so rapidly that word has barely reached the tribe's leaders elsewhere before the legions have arrived at Cenabum. The *praesidium* the Carnutes are attempting to prepare and dispatch will not be fast enough

5 Castrīs ante oppidum positīs diēī tempore exclūsus in
posterum oppugnātiōnem differt quaeque ad eam rem ūsuī
sint mīlitibus imperat 6 et, quod oppidum Cenabum pōns
flūminis Ligeris contingēbat, veritus nē noctū ex oppidō
profugerent, duās legiōnēs in armīs excubāre iubet.

---

differō, -ferre, distulī, dīlātus: postpone; disturb; vary
exclūdō, -ere, -ūsī, -ūsus: shut out, shut off; exclude
excubō (1): be watchful, keep vigil
Liger, Ligeris m.: the Loire
pōns, -tis m.: bridge
posterus, -a, -um: coming after, following, next
profugiō, fugere, fūgī, —: flee
vereor, -ērī, -itus: fear, dread; respect

---

castrīs: The construction of a *castra* every time the legions stopped was standard practice. With eight legions and an unknown number of cavalry and auxiliaries, Caesar's *castra* in this campaign were nearly as large as the *oppida* against which they were constructed. Even if very cramped, a *castra* for eight legions would have been hundreds of meters on a side

diēī tempore exclūsus: Caesar deemed it too late in the day to begin an assault; he postpones it *in posterum [diem]*

quaeque ad eam rem ūsuī sint mīlitibus imperat: *and he orders [to be prepared] the sorts of things which might be of use for the soldiers for this undertaking*; a double dative construction within a rel. clause of characteristic

vertitus nē: [*Caes.*] *having feared that*; *nē* introduces fear clause, with the inhabitants of the town as the implied subject

excubāre: The soldiers of the two chosen legions are ordered to remain fully armed and keep ready through the night as a rapid response force; the other legions can then take their rest in relative comfort. At 7.24.5 below, Caesar specifies that *duae legiōnēs prō castrīs excubābant*, clearly outside the walls of the *castra*, but in that instance the two legions are protecting ongoing work on the siege mound at the enemy's wall

7 Cenabensēs paulō ante mediam noctem silentiō ex oppidō ēgressī flūmen trānsīre coepērunt. Quā rē per explōrātōrēs nūntiātā Caesar legiōnēs 8 quās expedītās esse iusserat portīs incēnsīs intrōmittit atque oppidō potītur, perpaucīs ex hostium numerō dēsīderātīs quīn cūnctī caperentur, quod pontis atque itinerum angustiae multitūdinis fugam interclūserant. 9 Oppidum dīripit atque incendit, praedam mīlitibus dōnat, exercitum Ligerem trādūcit atque in Biturigum fīnēs pervēnit.

---

angustiae, -ārum f.pl.: narrowness
cūnctus, -a, um: all, every
dēsīderō (1): miss, lack; lose
dīripiō, -ere, -uī, -tus: tear apart; lay waste, plunder, pillage
dōnō (1): bestow, confer
ēgredior, -gredī, -gressus: go out
expedītus, -a, -um: ready, unencumbered; at hand
explōrātor, -ōris m.: scout, spy
interclūdō, -ere, -ūsī, -ūsus: cut off; blockade; hinder, block up
intrōmittō, -ere, -mīsī, -missus: send in; admit
perpaucus, -a, -um: very few
porta, -ae f.: gate
potior, -īrī, -ītus: get possession of, become master of (+ gen/abl)
praeda, -ae f.: loot, plunder

Cenabensēs: *the Cenabians*; *-ensis*, *-ense* is a typical Latin adjectival suffix
perpaucīs…dēsīderātis quīn cūnctī caperentur: in other words, with only a few stragglers getting away, the rest being captured alive (or killed); lit. "with only a few from the number of the enemy lacking from [a result that] every one of them be captured alive;" *quīn* can be used after verbs of lacking, resisting, refusing, delaying, and doubting, with a sense of "a result that"
pontis atque itinerum angustiae: the narrowness of the bridges and paths

[12] *Caesar and Vercingetorix approach near Noviodunum*

1 Vercingetorīx, ubi dē Caesaris adventū cognōvit, oppugnātiōne dēstitit atque obviam Caesarī proficīscitur.
2 Ille Noviodūnum oppugnāre īnstituerat. 3 Quō ex oppidō cum lēgātī ad eum vēnissent ōrātum ut sibi ignōsceret suaeque vītae cōnsuleret, ut celeritāte reliquās rēs cōnficeret quā plēraque erat cōnsecūtus, arma cōnferrī, equōs prōdūcī, obsidēs darī iubet.

---

celeritās, -tātis f.: speed, quickness
cōnsequor, -quī, -cūtus: follow, go/come after; attend on; pursue
cōnficiō, -ere, -fēcī, -fectus: make; prepare; complete
cōnsulō, -ere, -uī, -tus: (+ dat) consider, take care; ask advice
dēsistō, -ere, destitī, destitus: cease, desist (from) (+ abl); give up
ignōscō, -ere, ignōvī, ignōtus: pardon, forgive (+ dat)
lēgātus, -ī m.: (here) envoy, rep.
obviam: against; towards
plērus, -a, -um: (strengthened w/ *-que*) the majority, very many
prōdūcō, -ere, -dūxī, -ductus: lead forward, bring out; reveal

---

Ille: Caesar
Noviodūnum: Celtic "new fort" and the name of several *oppida*; this one was of the Bituriges, at modern Neung-sur-Beuvron
sibi: dative plur. masc. reflexive pronoun, *the townsfolk*
ōrātum: *to plead*; supine expressing purpose
ut celeritāte reliquās rēs cōnficeret, quā plēraque erat cōnsecūtus: *so that he might complete the remaining things with (the) speed with which he had pursued the majority [of his affairs]*; by heeding their pleas, Caesar could pursue his next goal with his characteristic *celeritās*

4 Parte iam obsidum trāditā, cum reliqua administrārentur, centuriōnibus et paucīs mīlitibus intrōmissīs quī arma iūmentaque conquīrerent, equitātus hostium procul vīsus est quī agmen Vercingetorīgis antecesserat. 5 Quem simul atque oppidānī cōnspexērunt atque in spem auxilī vēnērunt, clāmōre sublātō arma capere, portās claudere, mūrum complēre coepērunt.

---

administrō (1):, manage, handle, see to; assist;, conduct
agmen, -minis n.: (in Caes.) marching army, column, battle line; (elsewhere) herd, flock, crowd
claudō, -ere, clausī, clausus: close, shut, block up; conclude; blockade
compleō, -ēre, -ēvī, -ētus: fill (up); occupy, crowd
conquīrō, -ere, -quīsīvī, -quīsītus: seek out; investigate
intrōmittō, -ere, -mīsī, -missus: send in; admit
iūmentum, -ī n.: beast of burden
oppidānus, -ī m.: town inhabitant
procul: at distance, far off
spēs, -eī, f.: hope
tollō, tollere, sustulī, sublātus: lift, raise; destroy; remove, steal

---

centuriōnibus ... intrōmissīs quī ... conquīrerent: abl. absolute followed by relative clause of purpose
simul atque: *as soon as*; when *simul* precedes coordinate terms connected by *et, ac, atque*, or *et…et*, the sense is that the terms occur simultaneously
in spem auxilī vēnērunt: *entered into hope of aid;* render as "became hopeful for," a figurative use of *veniō* + *in* for metaphorical (emotional) movement

6 Centuriōnēs in oppidō, cum ex significātiōne Gallōrum novī aliquid ab eīs inīrī cōnsilī intellēxissent, gladiīs dēstrictīs portās occupāvērunt suōsque omnēs incolumēs recēpērunt.

---

dēstringō, -ere, -inxī, -ictus: unsheathe, draw; strip off
gladius, -iī m.: sword
incolumis, -e: unharmed, uninjured; alive, safe; unimpaired
novus, -a, -um: new, strange
porta, -ae f.: gate
significātiō, -iōnis f.: signal, outward sign; indication, meaning

---

novī aliquid ab eīs inīrī cōnsilī: *(that) something of a new plan was being undertaken by them;* ind. statement after *intellēxissent*

[13] *Caesar skirmishes with Vercingetorix and takes the town*

1 Caesar ex castrīs equitātum ēdūcī iubet, proelium equestre committit; labōrantibus iam suīs Germānōs equitēs circiter CCCC summittit quōs ab initiō habēre sēcum īnstituerat.
2 Eōrum impetum Gallī sustinēre nōn potuērunt atque in fugam coniectī multīs āmissīs sē ad agmen recēpērunt.

āmittō, -ere, -mīsī, -missus: lose; lose by death; send away, dismiss
circiter: about, approximately
coniciō, -ere, -iēcī, -iectus: cast, drive; throw together; conclude
ēdūcō, -ere, -dūxī, -ductus: lead out; draw up; bring up
equester, -tris, -tre: of cavalry
labōrō (1): labor, strive; struggle
summittō, -ere, -mīsī, -missus (= submittō): (here) send in support
sustineō, -ēre, -uī, -entus: endure, tolerate; support

---

labōrantibus iam suīs: *his men now struggling;* the *iam* indicates that time has moved forward from when the battle began, the narrative is now at his next action

Germanōs: By the middle of the 1st century BCE, Roman armies deployed very few Roman cavalry units, but instead relied on non-Roman auxiliary squadrons; during his military career Caesar regularly employed Gallic or Spanish cavalry supplied by Roman allies, or, as here, Germanic mercenaries, whose prowess on horseback was legendary. He had retained these 400 as a reserve and personal guard

summittit: *send up, send in*; *sub-* often connotes support or aid, e.g. *subsidium* (aid, reinforcement) or the sup- in Engl. "support" itself; c.f *BG* 4.26.4 (*quōs labōrantēs cōnspēxerat hīs subsidia submittēbat*) and *BG* 5.58.5 (*summittit cohortēs equitibus subsidiō*)

in fugam coniectī multīs āmissīs: *having been driven to flight with many lost*

Quibus prōflīgātīs rūrsus oppidānī perterritī comprehensōs eōs, quōrum operā plēbem concitātam exīstimābant, ad Caesarem perdūxērunt sēsēque eī dēdidērunt. 3 Quibus rēbus cōnfectīs, Caesar ad oppidum Avaricum quod erat maximum mūnītissimumque in fīnibus Biturigum atque agrī fertilissimā regiōne profectus est, quod eō oppidō receptō cīvitātem Biturigum sē in potestātem redāctūrum cōnfīdēbat.

---

comprehendō, -ere, -ī, -hensus: arrest, catch, seize, grasp firmly
concitō (1): rouse, incite, stir
cōnficiō, -ere, -fēcī, -fectus: make; prepare; complete
dēdō, -ere, -idī, -itus: give up, surrender; abandon (to); yield
mūnītus, -a, -um: defended, fortified; protected, secured, safe
oppidānus, -ī m.: townsperson
perdūcō, -ere, -ūxī, -uctus: lead, guide; prolong; induce, conduct
plēbs, plēbis, f.: the common folk, multitude, populace
potestās, -ātis f.: control, power, rule; strength, ability; chance
prōflīgō (1): overthrow, rout
redigō, -ere, redēgī, redāctus: reduce; render; lead back, bring
rūrsus: again; turned back; on the contrary, in return, in turn

---

quōrum operā: *by whose work;* with an implied *esse* connecting it to *plēbem concitātam*
perdūxērunt sēsēque eī dēdidērunt: the two verbs are parallel; the former controls the rest of the sentence. See Appendix A for a diagram of this passage
ad oppidum Avaricum...profectus est: Caesar plans the next phase of war: by capturing Avaricum, he thinks the Bituriges *sē in potestātem redāctūr*[*ōs*]
agrī: *of [their] country/land*

[14] *Vercingetorix calls a council of the Gauls*

1 Vercingetorīx tot continuīs incommodīs Vellaunodūnī, Cenabī, Noviodūnī acceptīs suōs ad concilium convocat.
2 Docet longē aliā ratiōne esse bellum gerendum atque anteā gestum sit. Omnibus modīs huic reī studendum ut pābulātiōne et commeātū Rōmānī prohibeantur. 3 Id esse facile quod equitātū ipsī abundent et quod annī tempore subleventur.

---

abundō (1): abound (in), have in large measure; overflow with
commeātus, -ūs m.: supplies
continuus, -a, -um: incessant, continuous, recurring; successive
incommodum, -ī n.: setback, detriment; defeat, disaster
pābulātiō, -iōnis f.: foraging
studeō, -ēre, -uī, —: (+ dat) be eager for, apply effort to
sublevō (1): lift up; support; assist
tot: so many

Vellaunodūnī, Cenabī, Noviodūnī: locatives
esse...gerendum: *must be waged;* passive periphrastic infinitive; begins an extended indirect statement, used throughout [14]
longē: *very much, entirely*
atque...gestum sit: *than [the war which] was waged in the past*; a rare use of *atque* (or its equivalent *ac*, *et*, or even more rarely *nisi* or *quam*) following *alius* in formal prose; in colloquial prose or in poetry, it is typically followed by an ablative of comparison instead. See A&G §407d
studendum: *[he says that] there must be a striving for the following circumstance* (huic res) *by all means available*; impersonal passive periphrastic infinitive; the following *ut* explains the circumstance

4 Pābulum secārī nōn posse; necessāriō dispersōs hostēs ex aedificiīs petere; hōs omnēs cotīdiē ab equitibus dēligī posse. 5 Praetereā salūtis causā reī familiāris commoda neglegenda: vīcōs atque aedificia incendī oportēre hōc spatiō ab viā quōque versus quō pābulandī causā adīre posse videantur.

---

aedificium, -iī n.: a building
commodum, -ī n.: interest, profits; convenience, advantage, benefit
cotīdiē: daily, every day
dēligō, -ere, -lēgī, -lēctus: single out; separate, remove
dīspergō, -ere, -ī, -sus: scatter, disperse
incendō, -ere, -ī, -sus: burn
necessāriō: inevitably, unavoidably
oportet, -ēre, -uit: (impersonal) require (to be done); ought
pābulor, -ārī, -ātus: forage, gather
pābulum, -ī n.: fodder, food
praetereā: in addition, further
salūs, -ūtis f.: health; prosperity
secō, -āre, -uī, sectus: cut off
versus: toward, in the direction of
vīcus, -ī m.: village, hamlet

---

pābulum...petere: given the time of year, the Romans will need to seek fodder from structures (barns, villages, etc.) scattered throughout the countryside
commoda: *the interests of private property;* neut. pl. nominative subject of *neglenda*
neglegenda: with implied *esse*; passive periphrastic
oportēre: *ought to, it is fitting to;* infin. as part of the extended indirect statement
hōc...quō: a correlative construction; Verc. is saying that the buildings and farms in range of Roman foraging parties must be burned
quōque versus: see note at 7.4.5

Hārum ipsīs rērum cōpiam suppetere, 6 quod quōrum in fīnibus bellum gerātur eōrum opibus subleventur. 7 Rōmānōs aut inopiam nōn lātūrōs aut māgnō perīculō longius ab castrīs prōcessūrōs, 8 neque interesse ipsōsne interficiant impedīmentīsne exuant, quibus āmissīs bellum gerī nōn possit.

āmittō, -ere, -mīsī, -missus: lose; lose by death; send away, dismiss
exuō, -ere, -ī, -tus: strip, deprive
impedīmentum, -ī n.: supplies
intersum, -esse, -fuī: make a difference; be of interest to
ops, -is f.: resources, aid
prōcēdō, -ere, -cessī, -cessus: go forward; advance, progress
sublevō (1): lift up; support; assist
suppetō, -ere, -īvī, -ītus: be at hand; be sufficient for

Hārum ipsīs rērum cōpiam: *an abundance of such resources for [the Gauls]*
eōrum opibus: *by the resources of whom*
lātūrōs, prōcessūrōs: sc. *esse*; future active infinitives continuing the extended ind. statement; *lātūrus* is fut. act. partic. from *ferre*, "will not endure"
magnō perīculō: *with great danger / very perilously*; abl. of manner
neque interesse: *nor does it make a difference [to the Gauls] whether…or*; a double question presented with the rare double enclitic *-ne…-ne*; more common is *utrum…an* or *-ne…an*; see A&G §334-35
ipsōs: the Romans, direct object of *interficiant / exuant*
quibus āmissīs: *with which (supplies) having been lost*; abl. abs.

9 Praetereā oppida incendī oportēre quae nōn mūnītiōne et locī nātūrā ab omnī sint perīculō tūta, neu suīs sint ad dētractandam mīlitiam receptācula neu Rōmānīs prōposita ad cōpiam commeātūs praedamque tollendam.

---

commeātus, -ūs m.: supplies
dētractō (1): evade; reduce
mīlitia, -ae f.: military service
mūnītiō, -is f.: fortification
necesse: necessary;, inevitable
praeda, -ae f.: loot, spoils
praetereā: in addition, further
prōpōnō, -ere, -posuī, -positus: offer; display; propose
receptāculum, -ī n.: refuge
tollō, -ere, sustulī, sublātus: (here) make off with, take away; (generally) raise up, build; destroy
tueor, -ī, tūtus: guard, protect; look at, behold, examine; regard

---

oppida: Caes. has used several words to refer to the structures of the Gauls which must be burned, from the *aedificia* and *vīcī* of 7.14.5 to the *oppida* here—any place which might contain supplies or harbor Gauls dodging conscription, from the humble farms and small hamlets to the largest towns
neu...neu: *so that...not...nor*; an *apocope* of *nēve* (the elision of a word-final vowel)*;* each *neu* clause lists a purpose for burning the *oppida quae nōn sint tūta*
receptācula sint...Rōmānīs prōposita [sint]: *that [the* oppida*] not become refuges...and not be offered up to the Romans*
suīs: *for our men*, i.e. Gauls attempting to avoid Verc.'s conscription efforts
ad dētractandam, ad tollendam: *for the purpose of*; gerundives

10 Haec sī gravia aut acerba videantur, multō illa gravius aestimāre: līberōs coniugēs in servitūtem abstrahī, ipsōs interficī, quae sit necesse accidere victīs.

---

abstrahō, -ere, -āxī, -actus: drag away, remove forcibly
acerbus, -a, -um: harsh; grievous
aestimō (1): value, assess; reckon
coniūnx, -iugis m./f.: spouse
gravis, -e: heavy; serious; severe
līberī, -ōrum m.: children
necesse: necessary;, inevitable
servitūs, -tūtis f.: slavery

---

multō: ablative of degree of difference with the comparative *gravius*
illa: *these following things*; accusative plural neuter
aestimāre: apodosis, translated as a present subjunctive; still an infinitive because of the extended indirect statement
līberōs coniugēs: subjects of *abstrahī* in the ind. statement with asyndeton; in the ancient world, slavery was a common fate for defeated peoples, especially in the Roman era. Though he seldom mentions it, Caesar's campaigns in Gaul resulted in the taking of tens of thousands of Gallic slaves, and there must have been robust logistics networks in place to transport them back to Italy and beyond
quae sit necesse accidere victīs: *which things [just listed] it is necessary to befall the defeated*

[15] *The Gauls debate the fate of Avaricum*

1 Omnium cōnsēnsū hāc sententiā probātā ūnō diē amplius XX urbēs Biturigum incenduntur. 2 Hoc idem fit in reliquīs cīvitātibus; in omnibus partibus incendia cōnspiciuntur, quae etsī magnō cum dolōre omnēs ferēbant, tamen hoc sibi sōlācī prōpōnēbant, quod sē prope explōrātā victōriā celeriter āmissa reciperātūrōs cōnfīdēbant.

āmittō, -ere, -īsī, -issus: lose; lose by death
cōnfīdō, -ere, -īsus: be assured, believe; rely on, trust (to)
cōnspiciō, -ere, -ēxī, -ectus: observe; notice; watch
dolor, -ōris m.: pain, grief
explōrō (1): bring forth, search out; investigate; prove, test
probō (1): to approve, commend
prope: nearly, almost
prōpōnō, -ere, -posuī, -positus: display, propose; declare, relate
reciperō (1): restore, recover
sōlācium, -iī n.: comfort, solace

---

cōnsēnsū...sententiā probātā...diē: three different ablative uses in succession—means, abl. absolute, and abl. of time within which
amplius XX urbēs: *more than 20 cities*; the use of *urbs* to refer to Gallic towns is unusual; this is the first occurrence in the *BG*. There will be a few more uses to come in *BG* VII
quae etsī...ferēbant: *which [burnings], although all were enduring [them]*
tamen hoc sibi sōlācī prōpōnēbant: *nevertheless they were relating to themselves this comfort*; *sōlāci* is a partitive gen., literally "this of a comfort"
prope explōrātā victōriā: *with victory nearly searched out*; abl. abs.
reciperātūrōs: *that they would restore*; fut. act. infinitive with implied *esse*

3 Dēlīberātur dē Avāricō in commūnī conciliō, incendī placēret an dēfendī. 4 Prōcumbunt omnibus Gallīs ad pedēs Biturigēs nē pulcherrimam prope tōtīus Galliae urbem, quae praesidiō et ōrnāmentō sit cīvitātī, suīs manibus succendere cōgerentur; 5 facile sē locī nātūrā dēfēnsūrōs dīcunt quod prope ex omnibus partibus flūmine et palūde circumdatā ūnum habeat et perangustum aditum.

---

aditus, -ūs, m.: approach, entrance
circumdō, -are, -dedī, -datus: surround; envelop, enclose
commūnis, -e: public
concilium, -ī, n.: council, meeting
dēlīberō (1): consider, ponder
palūs, -ūdis f.: swamp, marsh
perangustus, -a, -um: very narrow
placeō, -ēre, -uī, -itus: please, satisfy, give pleasure to (with dat)
prōcumbō, -ere, -cubuī, -cubitus: fall prostrate; sink, lie down
succendō, -ere, -ī, -cēnsus: set on fire, burn to the ground

---

dēlīberātur: *they ponder;* impersonal passive, lit. "there is a pondering"
incendī placēret an dēfendī: *whether it would be pleasing that [Avaricum] be burned or defended*; the *an* presents a double question
omnibus Gallīs ad pedēs: *at the feet of all the Gauls*; Latin shows possession with the dative here whereas English prefers the genitive
nē...cōgerentur: *begging that...*; the clause has the force of an indirect command after the implied pleading of the previous phrase; see Appendix A
quae praesidiō et ōrnāmentō sit cīvitātī: *which was both a guard and an ornament for the tribe*; double dative construction; verbs in subordinate clauses frequently (but not always) become subjunctive within extended indirect statements

6 Datur petentibus venia dissuādente prīmō Vercingetorīge, post concēdente et precibus ipsōrum et misericordiā vulgī. Dēfēnsōrēs oppidō idōneī dēliguntur.

---

dēfēnsor, -ōris m.: defender
dissuādeō, -ēre, -suāsī, -suāsus: dissuade, advise against
idōneus, -a, -um: suitable, fit
misericordia, -ae f.: pity, sympathy; compassion, mercy
prex, precis f.: prayer, request
venia, -ae f.: permission; favor, kindness; pardon
vulgus, -ī m.: the people, masses

---

petentibus: present act. participle, dative indirect object with *datur*
dissuādente prīmō...post concēdente: a double abl. abs. with *Vercingetorīge* as subject of both; note the contrasting *prīmō* and *post* to establish the sequence
precibus: abl. of cause

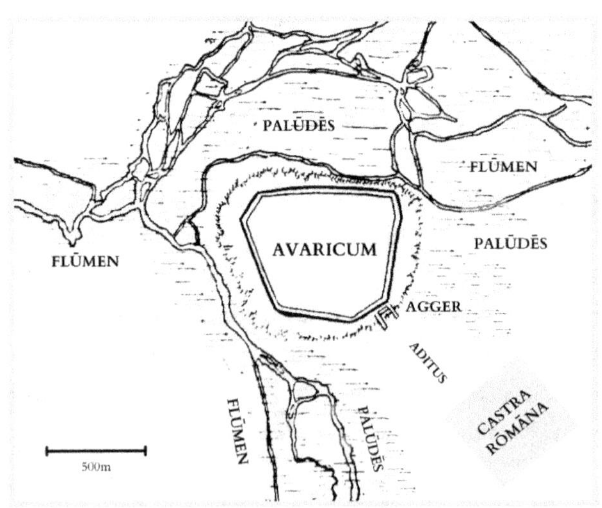

Gallī facile sē locī nātūrā dēfēnsūrōs dīcunt quod prope ex omnibus partibus flūmine et palūde circumdatā ūnum habeat et perangustum aditum (7.15.5)

[16] *Vercingetorix interferes with Roman foraging*

1 Vercingetorīx minōribus Caesarem itineribus subsequitur et locum castrīs dēligit palūdibus silvīsque mūnītum ab Avāricō longē mīlia passuum XVI. 2 Ibi per certōs explōrātōrēs in singula diēī tempora quae ad Avāricum agerentur cognōscēbat et quid fierī vellet imperābat.

---

certus, -a, -um: certain, reliable
dēligō, -ere, -lēgī, -lēctus: pick; choose, select, enroll
explōrātor, -ōris m.: scout
mūniō, -īre, -īvī, -ītus: fortify
prīmō: at first; in the first place
post: afterwards
silva, -ae f.: forest
subsequor, -ī, -secūtus: follow close after; pursue; support

---

in singula diēī tempora: *every hour of the day*
quid fierī vellet: *what he wished to be done;* ind. question introduced by *imperābat*

3 Omnēs nostrās pābulātiōnēs frūmentātiōnēsque observābat dispersōsque, cum longius necessāriō prōcēderent, adoriēbātur magnōque incommodō adficiēbat, etsī quantum ratiōne prōvidērī poterat, ab nostrīs occurrēbātur, ut incertīs temporibus dīversīsque itineribus īrētur.

---

adficiō, -ere, -fēcī, -fectus: affect, impair; influence; handle
adorior, -īrī, -ītus: assault, attack
dispergō, -ere, -sī, -sus: scatter
dīversus, -a, -um: different, unlike
frūmentātiō, -iōnis f.: foraging
incertus, -a, -um: uncertain; inconstant; variable
incommodum, -ī n.: harm, defeat; inconvenience; detriment
necessāriō: necessarily, inevitably
observō (1): watch, observe; heed
occurrō, -ere, -ī, -cursus: oppose, resist; come to mind
pābulātiō, -iōnis f.: fodder
prōcēdō, -ere, -cessī, -cessus: go forward; advance, progress
prōvideō, -ēre, -vīdī, -vīsus: foresee; provide for, make provision

---

pābulātiōnēs frūmentātiōnēsque: *foraging efforts [for fodder and for grain]*; men, horses, and draft animals all required a constant supply of food on the march
dispersōsque: sc. *nostrōs*; sc. *nostrī* for the following *prōcēderent*
cum: causal; Caes. is explaining why the Roman soldiers are *dispersōs*
etsī…īrētur: *although [this adversity] was being resisted by our men, as far as it was possible to be provided for by [the following] plan: that there was a departing at irregular times and by different routes*

[17] *The Romans build a camp, but struggle with lack of supplies*

1 Castrīs ad eam partem oppidī positīs Caesar quae intermissa ā flūmine et ā palūdibus aditum, ut suprā dīximus, angustum habēbat, aggerem apparāre, vīneās agere, turrēs duās cōnstituere coepit: nam circumvāllāre locī nātūra prohibēbat.
2 Dē rē frūmentāriā Boiōs atque Aeduōs adhortārī nōn dēstitit; quōrum alterī, quod nūllō studiō agēbant, nōn multum adiuvābant,

---

aditus, -us m.: approach, entrance
adiuvō (1): help, be of use
angustum, -ī n.: narrow place; passage, channel
apparō (1): prepare, make, equip
circumvāllō (1): blockade, invest
intermittō, -ere, -mīsī, -missus: neglect, leave off, leave unoccupied
studium, -iī n.: zeal, exertion
vīnea, -ae f.: covering, shelter, makeshift roof

---

intermissa: loosely, *having been left untouched by*; nom. sing. fem. modifying *quae;* Caes. explains that he put his *castra* at the spot which was not occluded by the river or by marshes
ut suprā dīximus: *as we mentioned above*; Caesar refers to himself in the 1st person here, a rarity. He described the physical setting of Avaricum back at 15.5
aggerem, vīneās, turrēs: typical structures created by a Roman army in a siege. The *agger* is a large ramp of dirt piled up adjacent to the defensive wall to lessen its height. The *vīneae* are temporary structures which protect the soldiers from projectiles while they work. The *turrēs* are tall movable wooden scaffolding towers on wheels, rollers, or sleds; when positioned next to a defensive wall, they permit soldiers to ascend and pass over the top. See also *BG* 3.21 for these methods
alterī...alterī: the Aedui and the Boii; see Appendix A

alterī nōn magnīs facultātibus, quod cīvitās erat exigua et īnfirma, celeriter quod habuērunt cōnsūmpsērunt. 3 Summā difficultāte reī frumentāriae adfectō exercitū tenuitāte Boiōrum, indīligentiā Aeduōrum, incendiīs aedificiōrum, ūsque eō ut complūrēs diēs frūmentō mīlitēs caruerint et pecore ex longinquiōribus vīcīs adāctō extrēmam famem sustentārent, nūlla tamen vōx est ab eīs audīta populī Rōmānī maiestāte et superiōribus victōriīs indigna.

---

adficiō, -ere, -fēcī, -fectus: affect, impair; influence; handle
adigō, -ere, -ēgī, -actus: drive, urge, force, compel; thrust
careō, -ēre, -uī, -itus: lack, be without (+ abl of separation)
(com)plūs, -plūris: very many
exiguus, -a, -um: small, paltry
facultās, -tātis f.: means; ability
famēs, -is f.: hunger
indignus, -a, -um: unworthy
indīligentia, -ae f.: negligence
īnfirmus, -a, -um: weak, fickle
longinquus, -a, -um: distant
maiestās, -tātis f.: dignity
pecus, pecoris n.: cattle, flock
sustineō, -ēre, -uī, -tentus: bear, withstand; keep back; uphold
tenuitās, -tātis f.: poverty, thinness
vīcus, vīci m.: village, quarter

---

adfectō exercitū: see Appendix A; the abl. abs. has adversative force ("although") answered eventually by *tamen*
ūsque eō ut: *[affected by difficulty] to such an extent that*, followed by result clause
complurēs diēs: *for many days*; accus. of duration of time
pecore...adāctō: *with cattle having been driven in*; abl. abs.
populī Rōmānī maiestāte et superiōribus victōriīs: abl. of respect

4 Quīn etiam Caesar cum in opere singulās legiōnēs appellāret et, sī acerbius inopiam ferrent, sē dīmissūrum oppugnātiōnem dīceret, ūniversī ab eō nē id faceret petēbant:
5 sīc sē complūrēs annōs illō imperante meruisse ut nūllam ignōminiam acciperent, nusquam īnfectā rē discēderent;

---

acerbus, -a, -um: harsh, grievous
appellō (1): call upon; address
dīmittō, -ere, -mīsī, -missus: dismiss, end; send away
ignōminia, -ae f.: dishonor
īnfectus, -a, -um: unfinished
mereō, -ēre, -uī, -itus: serve as soldier, render service; merit; incur
nusquam: (here) on no occasion
ūniversus, -a, -um: all together

Quīn etiam: *indeed; but...even*
acerbius: *too grieviously;* comp. adverb
sē dīmissūrum...dīceret: *he kept saying that he would end the siege*; sc. *esse*
nē id faceret: ind. command introduced by *petēbant*
sē...meruisse: an ind. statement explaining the contents of their plea
illō imperante: *with him [Caes.] commanding*, i.e. *under his command*
sīc...ut: *in such a manner...that*; introducing a result clause

6 hoc sē ignōminiae lātūrōs locō sī inceptam oppugnātiōnem relīquissent; 7 praestāre omnēs perferre acerbitātēs quam nōn cīvibus Rōmānīs quī Cenabī perfidiā Gallōrum interīssent parentārent. 8 Haec eadem centuriōnibus tribūnīsque mīlitum mandābant ut per eōs ad Caesarem dēferrentur.

---

acerbitās, -tātis f.: harshness, severity; bitterness; hardship
īdem, eadem, idem: the same
incipiō, -ere, -cēpī, -ceptus: begin, take in hand
intereō, -īre, -iī, itus: die; cease
mandō (1): entrust, pass word to; give order, command
parentō (1): propitiate (+ dat)
perferō, -ferre, -tulī, -lātus: suffer, endure to the end
perfidia, -ae f.: treachery
praestō, -āre, -stitī, -stitus: it is preferable, is better; stand out, be superior; show, manifest

---

hoc sē ignōminiae lātūrōs locō: *[they plead that they] would place/consider this in a position of dishonor*; the *hoc* seems to refer to the following *sī* clause
praestāre...quam: *they say that it is better...rather than*
parentārent: this word appears only here in Caesar. It is related to the *Parentalia* festival, when Romans made offerings to their ancestors. Caes.'s soldiers here wish to propitiate or honor the Roman citizens slain at Cenabum (*BG* 7.3.1) by not giving in; it can also mean "avenge the death of a parent"
Cenabī: *at Cenabum* (locative); see *BG* 7.3.1
haec eadem: *these same words*
centuriōnibus...dēferrentur: The normal line of communication was regular soldier to centurion/tribune to commander. Caesar is emphasizing here that he, like Alexander or Hannibal, is not above mingling with the rank and file and hearing their opinions. Thus he hears the same sentiment directly from the soldiers that he hears from the centurions and tribunes

[18] *The Gauls ambush Roman foragers*

1 Cum iam mūrō turrēs appropinquāssent, ex captīvīs Caesar cognōvit Vercingetorīgem cōnsūmptō pābulō castra mōvisse propius Avāricum atque ipsum cum equitātū expedītīsque, quī inter equitēs proeliārī cōnsuēssent, īnsidiārum causā eō profectum quō nostrōs posterō diē pābulātum ventūrōs arbitrārētur.

---

appropinquō (1): approach (+ dat)
cōnsuēscō, -ere, -suēvī, -suētus: be accustomed to, do by habit
expeditus, expeditī m.: scout, lightly-armed soldier
īnsidiae, -ārum f.: plot, ambush
pābulor, -ārī, -ātus: forage for food or fodder
pābulum, -ī n.: food, fodder
posterus, -a, -um: next, following
proelior, -ārī, ātus: fight, battle

1: for a basic diagram of this sentence, see Appendix A
appropinquāssent: -*quavissent*, syncopation
cōnsūmptō pābulō: abl. abs.; Verc. has destroyed all the foragable material in keeping with his plan to deny it to Roman forces
ipsum...prōfectum [esse]: *that he (Verc.) had departed*, continuing the ind. statement after *cognōvit*
profectum: *had set out; sc.* esse
causā: *for the purpose of, for the sake of*; usually with a gen. gerund(ive), but frequently only implied, as here
eō...quō: *to that place...where*
cōnsuēssent: -*suēvissent*, syncopation
ventūrōs: sc. *esse*
pābulātum: *to forage for food*; supine expressing purpose

2 Quibus rēbus cognitīs mediā nocte silentiō profectus ad
hostium castra māne pervēnit. 3 Illī celeriter per explōrātōrēs
adventū Caesaris cognitō carrōs impedīmentaque sua in
artiōrēs silvās abdidērunt, cōpiās omnēs in locō ēditō atque
apertō īnstrūxērunt. 4 Quā rē nūntiātā Caesar celeriter
sarcinās cōnferrī, arma expedīrī iussit.

---

abdō, -ere, -didī, -ditus: conceal; remove; go away
apertus, -a, -um: open, uncovered
artus, -a, -um: dense, narrow
carrus, -ī m.: wagon
ēditus, -a, -um: high, rising
expediō, -īre, -īvī, -ītus: procure, make ready; loosen; disengage
explōrātor, -ōris m.: scout, spy
impedīmentum, -ī n.: baggage
īnstruō, -ere, -strūxī, -strūctus: draw up; construct; prepare; fit out
māne: early in the morning
sarcina, -ae f.: soldier's kit; baggage, belongings
silva, -ae f.: forest

---

profectus: the subject is Caesar
silentiō: *in silence;* with adverbial force
illī: *the Gauls*
celeriter per explōrātōrēs adventū Caesaris cognitō: abl. abs.
carrōs impedīmentaque: both the Romans and the Gauls marched with supply trains that needed to be protected from opportunistic attack
sarcinās: Roman soldiers carried a huge variety of non-fighting items, including shovels, picks, axes, saws, stakes, tents, rope, chains, sacks, buckets, cooking pots, grinding mills, and food. These were in addition to fighting implements: *gladius* (sword), *pūgiō* (dagger), *scūtum* (shield), *pīla* (javelins), *galea* (helmet), *lorica* (armor), etc. In addition all these items were all the personal belongings and plunder (*sarcinae/impedimenta*), which might be left in a safe place if a more rapid marching pace was required

[19] *Caesar decides not to engage and explains why*

1 Collis erat lēniter ab īnfimō acclīvis. Hunc ex omnibus ferē partibus palūs difficilis atque impedīta cingēbat nōn lātior pedibus quīnquāgintā. 2 Hōc sē colle, interruptīs pontibus, Gallī fīdūciā locī continēbant, generātimque distribūtī in cīvitātēs, omnia vada ac saltūs eius palūdis obtinēbant, 3 sīc animō parātī, ut, sī eam palūdem Rōmānī perrumpere cōnārentur, haesitantēs premerent ex locō superiōre,

---

acclīvis, -e: rising, sloping; steep
cingō, -ere, cīnxī, cinctus: encircled, enclosed
collis, -is m.: hill
contineō, -ēre, -uī, -tentus: keep
fīdūcia, -ae f.: trust, confidence
generātim: by tribes, by kinds
haesitō (1): be stuck; hesitate
impedītus, -a, -um: inaccessible, difficult to pass
īnfimus, -a, -um: lowest
interrumpō, -ere, -ī, -ruptus: break up, break apart; interrupt
lātus, -a, -um: wide; spacious
lēniter: mildly, slightly
obtineō, -ēre, -uī, obtentus: hold, maintain, preserve; acquire
palūs, -ūdis f.: swamp, marsh
perrumpō, -ere, -rūpī, -ruptus: break through, force through
pōns, -tis m.: bridge
quīnquāgintā: fifty
saltus, -ūs m.: narrow passage
vadum, vadī n.: shallows, ford

---

lēniter ab īnfimō acclīvis: i.e, with a gentle rise, not steep; *īnfimō* is a substantive adjective for "the bottom"
2-3: for a basic diagram of this complicated sentence, see Appendix A
haesitantēs: *[the Romans] constantly getting stuck*; *haesitāre* is an iterative verb construction of *haerēre* "cling, adhere, hold fast; be fixed, firm; be at a loss;" the subject of *premerent* is the Gauls

ut quī propinquitātem locī vidēret parātōs prope aequō Mārte ad dīmicandum exīstimāret, quī inīquitātem condiciōnis perspiceret inānī simulātiōne sēsē ostentāre cognōsceret. 4 Indignantēs mīlitēs Caesar, quod cōnspectum suum hostēs perferre possent tantulō spatiō interiectō, et signum proelī exposcentēs ēdocet,

---

aequus, -a, -um: even, equal
condiciō, -iōnis f.: situation; manner; stipulation
cōnspectus, -ūs m.: view, sight
dīmicō (1): struggle, be in peril
ēdoceō, -ēre, -cuī, -tus: inform (thoroughly), apprise, prove
exposcō, -ere, -poposcī: request; demand
inānis, -e: empty, hollow
intericiō,-ere, -iēcī, -iectus: set between; intersperse
Mārs, Mārtis m.: Mars (Roman god of war); fighting, battle
propinquitās, -tātis f.: nearness
simulātiō, -iōnis f.: imitation, pretense, deceit; assumption
tantulus, -a, -um: so small

---

ut quī...quī: *with the result that anyone who...[but] anyone who...*
parātōs prope aequō Mārte ad dīmicandum: *prepared for fighting in almost equal battle*; Mārte here is metonymy for the general act of fighting
exīstimāret: the object is the Gauls and the Romans
inānī simulātiōne sēsē ostentāre: *that they were displaying an empty imitation*; Caesar means that an observer would think that the Gauls are positioned such that any battles will occur on equal terms (even though close observation will reveal the Gauls' upper hand). From the perspective of the Roman soldier, this situation seems acceptable, but Caesar here indicates his superior evaluative skills
exposcentēs: parallel with *indignantēs*, both modifying *mīlitēs [Rōmānōs]*
4-5: see Appendix A for a basic diagram of this sentence

quantō dētrīmentō et quot virōrum fortium morte necesse sit
cōnstāre victōriam; quōs cum sīc animō parātōs videat 5 ut
nūllum prō suā laude perīculum recūsent, summae sē
inīquitātis condemnārī dēbēre nisi eōrum vītam suā salūte
habeat cāriōrem. 6 Sīc mīlitēs cōnsōlātus eōdem diē redūcit in
castra reliquaque quae ad oppugnātiōnem pertinēbant oppidī
administrāre īnstituit.

---

condemnō (1): find guilty
cōnsōlor, -āri, -ātus: encourage, comfort; alleviate, soothe
cōnstō, -āre, -itī, -ātus: cost (+ abl); be certain; be determined; be extant, consist of
inīquitās, -tātis f.: unfairness
mors, mortis f.: death
pertineō, -ēre, -uī: reach; relate/pertain to
recūsō (1): decline, reject, refuse

---

quantō dētrīmentō...quot morte...necesse sit cōnstāre victōriam: *how much damage...the death of how many...it would be necessary that victory cost*
quōs cum: introduces a circumstantial clause; the antecedent of *quos* is the Roman soldiers
sē...dēbēre: sc. *ēdocet* from above
nisi eōrum vītam suā salūte habeat cāriōrem: *if he did not consider their life more precious than his own safety*; the verbs *habēre* and *ducere* can often have this meaning "consider" with a predicate

[20] *Vercingetorix replies to his detractors*

1 Vercingetorīx, cum ad suōs redīsset, prōditiōnis īnsimulātus, quod castra propius Rōmānōs mōvisset, quod cum omnī equitātū discessisset, quod sine imperiō tantās cōpiās relīquisset, quod eius discessū Rōmānī tantā opportūnitāte et celeritāte vēnissent; 2 nōn haec omnia fortuitō aut sine cōnsiliō accidere potuisse; rēgnum illum Galliae mālle Caesaris concessū quam ipsōrum habēre beneficiō.

---

beneficium, -iī n.: favor; honor, distinction
concessus, -ūs m.: permission
fortuitō: accidentally, by chance
īnsimulō (1): accuse, charge; allege
mālō, mālle, māluī: prefer
opportūnitās, -tātis f.: convenience, advantage
prōditiō, -ōnis f.: treason, betrayal
prope: near, nearly; close by; almost
rēgnum, -ī n.: kingship, rule; domain, a kingdom

īnsimulātus: sc. *est* to form a perfect passive indicative; see Appendix A
quod: *[due to] the fact that;* this is a difficult passage: the subjunctives are of "alleged reason" and convey the stated grounds for an assertion ("on the grounds that he had…"); the actuality of the actions (moving the camp, departing with the cavalry, etc) are not in question
sine imperiō: *without a leader;* it seems that Verc. failed to delegate authority
discessū: *due to his [Verc.'s] departure,* or perhaps *during his departure*
opportūnitāte…fortuitō: the Gauls allege that Verc.'s departure was a little *too* conveniently timed with the Roman attack on their camp
potuisse, mālle: infinitives in an implied indirect statement; sc. "*the accusing Gauls say that;*" for *mālle*, sc. *Vercingetorīgem* as subject
concessū: *through the permission of*

3 Tālī modō accūsātus ad haec respondit: quod castra mōvisset, factum inopiā pābulī etiam ipsīs hortantibus; quod propius Rōmānōs accessisset, persuāsum locī opportūnitāte, quī sē ipsum mūnītiōne dēfenderet; 4 equitum vērō operam neque in locō palūstrī dēsīderārī dēbuisse et illīc fuisse ūtilem quō sint profectī; 5 summam imperiī sē cōnsultō nūllī discēdentem trādidisse nē is multitūdinis studiō ad dīmicandum impellerētur, cui reī propter animī mollitiem studēre omnēs vidēret, quod diūtius labōrem ferre nōn possent;

---

cōnsultō: deliberately, intentionally
dēsīderō (1): want, wish for, require; (in pass.) miss, lack
dīmicō (1): struggle, be in peril
diūtius: longer, for a longer time
illīc: in that place, yonder
impellō, -ere, -pulī, -pulsus: drive, push on; urge on; induce
inopia, -ae f.: lack, need, dearth
mollitiēs, -ieī f.: softness, weakness
mūnītiō, -iōnis f.: fortification
opportūnitās, -tātis f.: convenience, advantage
pābulum, -ī n.: food; fodder
palūster, –stris, –stre: swampy
persuadeō, -ēre, -suāsī, -suāsus: (here) induce, prompt
quō: (to) where
studium, -iī n.: zeal, exertion
tālis, -e: such, of such a sort
ūtilis, -e: useful

---

quod…factum: *with regard to the fact that…[he says that] it was done*
factum, persuāsum: sc. *esse* in extended ind. statement
etiam ipsīs hortantibus: the Gauls themselves had even urged this move
5: see Appendix A for a short diagram of this section
summam imperiī: that is, the command of the Gauls in his absence
is: that is, the person to whom he might have delegated command

6 Rōmānī sī cāsū intervēnerint, fortūnae, sī alicuius indiciō vocātī, huic habendam grātiam, quod et paucitātem eōrum ex locō superiōre cognōscere et virtūtem dēspicere potuerint quī dīmicāre nōn ausī turpiter sē in castra recēperint.
7 Imperium sē ab Caesare per prōditiōnem nūllum dēsīderāre, quod habēre victōriā posset quae iam esset sibi atque omnibus Gallīs explōrāta: quīn etiam ipsīs remittere, sī sibi magis honōrem tribuere quam ab sē salūtem accipere videantur.

---

audeō, -ēre, ausus: dare
casus, casūs m.: chance; accident; calamity, fall
dēspiciō, -ere, -spēxī, -spectus: look down on; disdain, despise
dēsīderō (1): want, wish for, require; (in pass.) miss, lack
explōrō (1): bring/search out; investigate, test
grātia, -ae f.: gratitude; favor
indicium, -iī n.: information, disclosure; evidence, proof
interveniō, -īre, -vēnī, -ventus: come between; occur, pop up
paucitās, -tātis f.: scarcity, fewness
prōditiō, -ōnis f.: betrayal, treason
tribuō, -ere, -uī, -ūtus: grant, allot
turpiter: repulsively, disgracefully, shamelessly

---

sī...sī...habendam grātiam: see Appendix A for a diagram of this tricky passage. Instead of being a problem, the arrival of the Romans in his absence is fortuitous, which is then explained further (*quod*)
alicuius indiciō: *by the disclosure of some [spy/traitor]*
turpiter: Caesar's characterization of his actions, here in Verc.'s words, contrasts with his own analysis of the event in the previous chapter
quīn...videantur: *[he says that] in fact he would even hand back [his leadership], if [the Gauls] seemed to bestow honor* ***on*** *him rather than take safety* ***from*** *him*

8 “Haec ut intellegātis” inquit “ā mē sincērē prōnūntiārī,
audītē Rōmānōs mīlitēs.” 9 Prōdūcit servōs quōs in
pābulātiōne paucīs ante diēbus excēperat et fame vinculīsque
excruciāverat. Hī iam ante ēdoctī quae interrogātī
prōnūntiārent, 10 mīlitēs sē esse legiōnāriōs dīcunt; fame et
inopiā adductōs clam ex castrīs exīsse sī quid frūmentī aut
pecoris in agrīs reperīre possent;

---

clam: secretly; covertly
ēdoceō, -ēre, -uī, -tus: instruct
excruciō (1): torture; torment
famēs, -is f.: hunger, want
pābulātiō, -iōnis f.: foraging
pecus, pecoris n.: herd; flock
prōdūcō, -ere, -dūxī, -ductus: lead forward, bring out, reveal
reperiō, -īre, -ī, -pertus: discover, obtain; learn
salūs, salūtis f.: health; prosperity
sincērē: candidly; honestly
vinculum, -ī n.: chain, prison

---

servōs: Caesar clearly terms them slaves, suggesting they were not in fact soldiers. These slaves would have accompanied the Roman soldiers in their foraging. Caesar might also be deliberately downplaying the status of these captives if they were in fact legionnaires

iam ante ēdoctī: *having been instructed before now*; Verc. has carefully coached these “witnesses” to ensure they say what he wishes

sī quid...possent: *[to determine] if they might be able to discover anything*

11 similī omnem exercitum inopiā premī, nec iam vīrēs sufficere cuiusquam nec ferre operis labōrem posse: itaque statuisse imperātōrem, sī nihil in oppugnātiōne oppidī prōfēcissent, trīduō exercitum dēdūcere. "Haec," inquit, "ā mē," Vercingetorīx, "beneficia habētis, 12 quem prōditiōnis īnsimulātis; cuius operā sine vestrō sanguine tantum exercitum victōrem fame cōnsūmptum vidētis; quem turpiter sē ex fugā recipientem nē quā cīvitās suīs fīnibus recipiat ā mē prōvīsum est."

īnsimulō (1): accuse, charge; allege
nihil: nothing; in no way; not at all
prōditiō, -ōnis f.: betrayal, treason
prōficiō, -ere, -fēcī, -fectus: make progress, advance; have success
prōvideō, -ēre, -vīdī, -vīsus: discern; foresee; see to; avert
quisquam, quidquam: anyone
statuō, -ere, -uī, -tūtus: set up, establish, set; decide, think
sufficiō, -ere, -fēcī, -fectus: be sufficient, adequate
trīduum, trīduī n.: three days
turpiter: disgracefully, shamelessly
vīs, vīs f.: violence, potency; (in pl.) physical strength

---

statuisse imperātōrem: *[they say that] their commander [Caes.] had decided that*
inquit: *ōrātiō rēcta* is relatively rare in the *commentāriī*, but most prevalent in book VII; for speeches in Caes., see Grillo's discussion in *The Cambridge Companion to the Writings of Julius Caesar* (2017)
quem...cuius...quem: the first two pronouns refer to himself (Verc.), while the final *quem* has *exercitum* as its antecedent
cuius operā: *because of the work/efforts of whom*
ā mē prōvīsum est: *it has been seen to/arranged by me [that]*
nē quā...recipiat: *that no [Gallic] tribe receive which [army] within its borders*

[21] *The Gauls approve of Vercingetorix and send support*

1 Conclāmat omnis multitūdō et suō mōre armīs concrepat, quod facere in eō cōnsuērunt cuius ōrātiōnem approbant. Summum esse Vercingetorīgem ducem, nec dē eius fide dubitandum, nec maiōre ratiōne bellum administrārī posse.
2 Statuunt ut X mīlia hominum dēlēcta ex omnibus cōpiīs in oppidum mittantur, 3 nec sōlīs Biturigibus commūnem salūtem committendam cēnsent, quod paene in eō, sī id oppidum retinuissent, summam victōriae cōnstāre intellegēbant.

---

approbō (1): approve, favor
conclāmō (1): shout together
concrepō, -āre, -uī, -itus: clash, creak, rattle, make noise
cēnseō, -ēre, -uī, –sus: judge, determine, be of the opinion
committō, -ere, -mīsī, -missus: entrust to; enter on, engage in
cōnstō, -āre, -itī, -ātus: (here) consist of, rest/stand on
cōnsuēsco, -ere, -suēvī, -suētus: be accustomed to, have habit of
dēligō, -ere, -ēgī, -lēctus: select
mōs, mōris m.: habit, custom
retineō, -ēre, -uī, -tentus: hold fast, preserve; restrain
sōlus, -a, -um: only, alone
statuō, -ere, -uī, -ūtus: decide, determine; erect; support

---

nec dē eius fide dubitandum: *nor must there be doubt of his honor*
in eō: *in the following*; that is, that they keep possession of the town
summam victoriae: in the past, this section has been interpreted to mean that the Gauls did not wish the Bit. alone to receive all the glory of the defense. It seems more accurate, however, to read it as the Gauls' unwillingness to *rely* on the Bit. alone for the defense, since it was such a key element in their strategy

[22] *Caesar describes Gallic battlefield technology*

1 Singulārī mīlitum nostrōrum virtūtī cōnsilia cuiusque modī Gallōrum occurrēbant, ut est summae genus sollertiae atque ad omnia imitanda et efficienda quae ab quōque trāduntur aptissimum.

---

aptus, -a, -um: suitable; adapted; comfortable
efficiō, -ere, -fēcī, -fectus: cause, bring about; accomplish
genus, generis n.: type, kind, race
imitor, -ārī, -ātus: copy, mimic
occurrō, -ere, -ī, -rsus: (+ dat) meet, oppose, resist; clash with
quisque, quidque: each, every
singulāris, -e: unique; remarkable
sollertia, -ae f.: skill, cleverness; resourcefulness

---

singulārī...occurrēbant: the subject *cōnsilia* is delayed, and the verb takes a dative object; Caes. contrasts the *virtūs* of the Romans with the technological response of the Gaul, a reversal of the typical attributes of the two sides in *BG*
cuiusque modī: *of every kind*
genus...aptissimum: *a type (of society) very suited to/for* or *very comfortable with* (+*ad* and gerundive); Caesar typically uses the term *genus* to denote broad category types. At *BG* 4.20.1 he seeks to know what *genus* of men dwell in Britain; at *BG* 6.28 he uses the word to indicate socio-economic types among Gauls; elsewhere he uses it for types of fighting (employed by Germans, *BG* 1.48.5; of Britons fighting from chariots, *BG* 4.33.1; of types of *cunīculī*, *BG* 7.22.2 below)
ab quōque: *by anyone*

2 Nam et laqueīs falcēs āvertēbant quās cum dēstināverant tormentīs intrōrsus redūcēbant, et aggerem cunīculīs subtrahēbant, eō scientius quod apud eōs magnae sunt ferrāriae atque omne genus cunīculōrum nōtum atque ūsitātum est.

---

cunīculus, -ī m.: hole, mineshaft
destinō (1): fasten down; mark out; fix in mind; aim
ferrāria, -ae f.: iron mine
intrōrsus: (to) within, inwards
pariō, -ere, peperī, partus: bear; give birth to; beget, bring forth
sciēns, scientis: knowing, skilled
subtrahō, -ere, -trāxī, -trāctus: remove from below, carry off; take away; undermine
ūsitātus, -a, -um: familiar, everyday; customary, usual

---

laqueīs falcēs āvertēbant: *they turn away the hooks with snares*; the *laqueus* is simply a loop on a rope, and a *falx* is a hook on a long pole used by Roman soldiers to pull away parts of a wall or the men stationed upon it; see *BG* 3.14.5; Tacitus *Hist.* 3.27

quās...tormentīs intrōrsus redūcēbant: *which...they were bringing back within the walls by machines*; the term *tormentum* is applied in Latin to a variety of torsion-based devices, including projectile-hurlers (typical in Roman armies), torture racks, and even clothes-presses. Here Caes. seems to mean that the Gauls have devised a winch of some sort to lasso and then pull away the *falcēs*

cunīculīs: a *cunīculus* is a rabbit, from the Greek κύνικλος, but by extension means, as result of their burrowing, "underground passage, hole, cavity." Here they are the tunnels created by soldiers digging under fortifications in an attempt to compromise them; see *BG* 3.21.2-3 and 7.24.2 below, and Livy 5.19.10; 31.17.2; 38.7.6

aggerem: a siege mound; see the note at *BG* 7.17.1 above

eō scientius quod: *the more skillfully [they employ the tunnels] because*; ablative of degree of difference with comparative adverb

3 Tōtum autem mūrum ex omnī parte turribus contabulāverant atque hās coriīs intēxerant. 4 Tum crēbrīs diurnīs nocturnīsque ēruptiōnibus aut aggerī ignem īnferēbant aut mīlitēs occupātōs in opere adoriēbantur, et nostrārum turrium altitūdinem, quantum hās cotīdiānus agger expresserat,

---

adorior, -īrī, -ītus: assault, attack
contabulō (1): build in tiers/stories
corium, coriī n.: skin, hide
cotīdiānus, -a, -um: daily
crēber, -bra, -brum: thick, pressed together; frequent; abundant
diurnus, -a, -um: by day
ēruptiō, -iōnis f.: sudden rush of troops from a position; a sally
exprimō, -ere, -pressī, -pressus: squeeze/press/thrust out
īnferō, -ferre, -tulī, -lātus: (w/ fire) throw upon, set
integō, -ere, -tēxī, -tēctus: cover
nocturnus, -a, -um: at night
turris, -is f.: tower, turret, siege machine

---

murum...turribus contabulāverant: the verb *contabulāre* has multiple meanings, but here seems to mean that the Gauls had created tiers or stories on the defensive walls of the town by means of elevated turrets; elsewhere the verb means to furnish or cover with boards (*BG* 5.40; Livy 24.37.7; cf. Suet. *Calig.* 19)

coriīs intēxerant: the *coria* were hide coverings for the *turrēs* which helped protect them from flaming projectiles, and were generally used both on walls and on siege machinery

mīlitēs occupātōs: [*Rōmānōs*]

quantum hās cotīdiānus agger expresserat: *as much as the ramp/mound had daily thrust out* (perhaps *inched forward*) *these (siege towers)*; the primary purpose of the ramp was to provide a method to raise the siege towers to the height of the wall

commissīs suārum turrium mālīs adaequābant, et apertōs cunīculōs praeustā et praeacūtā māteriā et pice fervefactā et maximī ponderis saxīs morābantur moenibusque appropinquāre prohibēbant.

---

adaequō (1): make equal in height, come up to level; compare (to)
apertus, -a, -um: open; uncovered, exposed; manifest
appropinquō (1): (+ dat) approach, come near to; draw nigh
cunīculus, -ī m.: hole, mineshaft
fervefactus, -a, -um: hot; melted
mālus, -ī m.: beam; tall pole
māteria, -ae f.: wood, timber
moenia, -ium n.: town walls
moror, -ārī, ātus: delay; stay
pix, picis f.: pitch, tar
pondus, -eris n.: weight, mass
praeacūtus, -a, -um: sharpened
praeustus, -a, -um: burnt at the end; hardened by burning

---

commissīs suārum turrium mālīs: *wooden beams having been joined to their own towers*; the Gauls continually increase the height of their own *turrēs* in response
apertōs cunīculōs: it is not known what Caes. means here. These could be Roman tunnels very similar to those attempted by the Gauls, in which case *apertōs* would be the perfect passive participle of *aperīre* "laid bare, rendered accessible, discovered," presumably by their own counter-tunneling efforts and then assailed with *māteriā et saxīs*; or these *cunīculī* could be open trenches (adj. *apertī*, favored here), involved in some way with the construction of the *agger*, or perhaps less literal "passageways" atop the *agger* which were covered by *vīneae*. In either case, it is not clear what use the *māteriae* would be—the burning pitch and stones are more obvious in their usage and effectiveness
fervefactā: a relatively rare term in Latin, found only twice in *BG*, once each in culinary contexts in Columella and Apicus, but frequently in Pliny *NH*
morābantur, prohibēbant: conative imperfects: *were attempting to delay, prevent*

[23] *Caesar describes the method of Gallic wall construction*

1 Mūrī autem omnēs Gallicī hāc ferē fōrmā sunt. Trabēs dērēctae perpetuae in longitūdinem paribus intervāllīs, dīstantēs inter sē bīnōs pedēs, in solō collocantur. 2 Hae revinciuntur intrōrsus et multō aggere vestiuntur;

---

agger, aggeris m.: (here) dirt
bīnī, -ae, -a: two by two; two to each; two at a time
colloco (1): arrange, place together, set up, erect
dērēctus, -a, -um: straight
dīstāns, -ntis: distant; separate
intervāllum, -ī n.: an intermediate space; (of time) an interval
intrōrsus: (to) within, inwards
longitūdō, -dinis f.: length
mūrus, -ī m.: wall
par, paris: equal
perpetuus, -a, -um: continuous
solum, solī n.: bottom, ground
revinciō, -īre, -xī, -ctus: fasten
trabs, trabis f.: beam, timber; log
vestiō, -īre, -īvī, -ītus: cover

---

hāc ferē formā: This chapter is highly technical Latin and, like Caesar's attempt to describe his bridge across the Rhine (*BG* 4.17.3-9), sometimes difficult to follow

mūrus: Caes. uses *mūrus* and *moenia* interchangeably; *moenia*, almost always plural, might be translated as "fortifications; ramparts," while the *mūrus* is the wall itself

in longitūdinem: *lengthwise / end-to-end*

ea autem, quae dīximus, inter vālla grandibus in fronte saxīs effarciuntur. 3 Hīs collocātis et coagmentātis alius īnsuper ōrdō additur, ut idem illud intervāllum servētur neque inter sē contingant trabēs, sed paribus intermissae spatiīs singulae singulīs saxīs interiectīs arte contineantur.

---

addō, -ere, -didī, -ditus: add, place in addition, attach to
ars, artis f.: skill
coagmentō (1): join, connect
effarciō, -īre, -fertus: fill out; cram
frōns, -ontis f.: front, façade; exterior; (elsewhere) brow, face
grandis, -e: large, great, grand
īnsuper: above, on top; in addition
intericiō, -ere, -iēcī, -iectus: intersperse, insert; throw between
intermittō, -ere, -mīsī, -missus: leave off, omit, interrupt; let pass
ōrdō, -inis m.: line, row, series
vāllum, -ī n.: rampart; entrenchment

---

alius īnsuper ōrdō: *another row [of* trabēs*] above*
paribus...spatiīs: from the outside and the inside, the facing of the wall would show the regularly-spaced ends of the beams, placed perpendicular to the course of the wall and seeming to float in regular intervals among a smooth facing of stones (see illustration on p.75 below). Between the two wall facings, the unseen interior structure of these perpendicular beams is reinforced by long beams placed at right angles (parallel with the course of the wall), attached to the perpendicular beams by morticed joints, and the whole interior is filled with soil and/or rubble. This type of construction is termed *murus Gallicus* and is typical of Iron Age *oppida* in western Europe during the *La Tène* period. Several examples of the technique have been excavated, mostly in France, and some site curators have created partial constructions (as at Bibracte, *oppidum* of the Aedui, near modern Autun)

4 Sīc deinceps omne opus contexitur dum iūsta mūrī altitūdō expleātur. 5 Hoc cum in speciem varietātemque opus dēfōrme nōn est alternīs trabibus ac saxīs, quae rēctīs līneīs suōs ōrdinēs servant, tum ad ūtilitātem et dēfēnsiōnem urbium summam habet opportūnitātem, quod et ab incendiō lapis et ab ariete māteria dēfendit, quae perpetuīs trabibus pedēs quadrāgēnōs plērumque intrōrsus revincta neque perrumpī neque distrahī potest.

---

ariēs, -etis m.: (here) battering ram
contexō, -ere, -uī, -tus: join, bind, weave; construct, put together
dēfōrmis, -e: ugly, deformed
deinceps: in order, successively
distrahō, -ere, -trāxī, -tractus: draw apart, rend, separate
expleō, -ēre, -plēvī, -plētus: fill out; complete, finish
incendium, -iī n.: fire
intrōrsus: (to) within, inwards
lapis, lapidis m.: stone
līnea, -ae f.: line, mark; string
māteria, -ae f.: wood, timber
ōrdō, -inis m.: line, row, series
perrumpō, -ere, -rūpī, -ruptus: break through
quadrāgēnus, -a, -um: forty each
rēctus, -a, -um: straight
revinciō, -īre, -xī, -ctus: fasten
speciēs, -iēī f.: sight, appearance
trabs, trabis f.: beam, timber; log
ūtilitās, -tātis f.: usefulness
varietās, -tātis f.: difference; varied appearance

---

omne opus: *the whole work, the whole wall*
dum iūsta mūrī altitūdō expleātur: *until the proper height of the wall be finished*
cum…tum: *not only…but also*
revincta: as described in the note of the previous section, the *trabēs* are reinforced on the interior of the wall with further beams set at right angles, which joins the whole length together

[24] *The Gauls attack the Roman siege machines*

1 Hīs tot rēbus impedītā oppūgnātiōne mīlitēs, cum tōtō tempore frīgore et assiduīs imbribus tardārentur, tamen continentī labōre omnia haec superāvērunt et diēbus XXV aggerem lātum pedēs CCCXXX, altum pedēs LXXX exstrūxērunt.

---

assiduus, -a, -um: constant
continēns, -entis: continual, uninterrupted; limiting
exstruō, -ere, -ūxī, -ctus: build up, raise, build, construct
frīgus, -oris n.: cold; winter
imber, imbris m.: rain
impediō, -īre, -īvī, -ītus: hinder, impede, obstruct, prevent from
tardō (1): slow, delay, impede

---

tōtō tempore: *the entire time*; abl. of duration of time, instead of the accusative; cf *BC* 1.46: *hōc cum esset modō pugnātum continenter horīs quinque*

aggerem lātum pedēs CCCXXX, altum pedēs LXXX: *they built the ramp to be 330 feet wide, 80 feet tall.* The great width was perhaps due to the necessity to support two massive siege towers (*turrēs*) next to each other, though some doubt these numbers. Such a height would be necessary if the walls of the town were fronted by a deep moat. Caes. utilized an *agger* a total of five times in the Gallic Wars: the first at Noviodunum, *oppidum* of the Suessiones (*BG* 2.12.1-5) and second against the Atuatuci (*BG* 2.30-33), both in 57 BCE; the third, via his legate P. Crassus, against the stronghold of the Sotiates in 56 (*BG* 3.21-22); the fourth here at Avaricum in 52; and the fifth at Uxellodunum, which has the most detailed description (*BG* 8.41-44). There are surviving Roman examples of *aggerēs* at Dura-Europos on the Euphrates and at Masada in the Judaean Desert. See S. Krausz, "Julius Caesar's assault ramp at the *Oppidum* of *Avaricum* in 52 BC" in *Enclosing Space, Opening New Ground - Iron Age Studies from Scotland to Mainland Europe*, ed. Romankiewicz, Fernández-Götz, Lock, and Buchsenschütz (Oxbow 2019), 23-31

2 Cum is mūrum hostium paene contingeret et Caesar ad opus cōnsuētūdine excubāret mīlitēsque hortārētur nē quod omnīnō tempus ab opere intermitterētur, paulō ante tertiam vigiliam est animadversum fūmāre aggerem quem cunīculō hostēs succenderant. 3 Eōdemque tempore tōtō mūrō clāmōre sublātō duābus portīs ab utrōque latere turrium ēruptiō fiebat.

---

cōnsuētūdō, -dinis f.: habit, custom; tradition, precedent
cunīculus, -ī m.: hole, mineshaft
ēruptiō, -iōnis f.: sudden rush of troops from a position; a sally
excubō (1): keep watch, be vigilant; camp out
fumō (1): smoke
intermittō, -ere, -mīsī, -missus: leave off, omit, interrupt; let pass
latus, lateris n.: side, flank
omnīnō: at all
paene: nearly, almost
succendō, -ere, -ī, -cēnsus: set on fire from below
uter-, utra-, utrumque: each (of two)

---

ad opus cōnsuētūdine excubāret: *was watching over the work as usual*
nē quod…tempus: *that not any time*; indirect command after *hortārētur*; remember: "after *si, nisi, num* or *nē,* all the *ali-* drop away"
paulō ante tertiam vigiliam: *a little while before the third watch;* the third watch was from midnight to 3 AM, so this incident took place a little before midnight
cunīculō: ablative of means; see the note at 22.2
ēruptiō fiebat: *a sally happened/arose*; a sally is a sudden attack from within the defenses of a besieged place

4 Aliī facēs atque āridam māteriem dē mūrō in aggerem ēminus iaciēbant, picem reliquāsque rēs quibus ignis excitārī potest fundēbant ut quō prīmum currerētur aut cui reī ferrētur auxilium vix ratiō inīrī posset.

āridus, -a, -um: dry, parched
ēminus: from a distance
excitō (1): (here) kindle, light
fax, facis f.: torch, firebrand
fundō, -ere, fūdī, fūsus: pour
iaciō, -ere, iēcī, iactus: throw
ignis, -is m.: fire
ineō, inīre: (here) begin, undertake
māteriēs, -ieī f.: = *māteria, -ae,* material; wood
pix, picis f.: pitch, tar
quō: (to) where
vix: hardly, scarcely, barely

Aliī...iaciēbant...[aliī] fundēbant: *some men were throwing...some men were pouring*; typically a second *aliī* would be expected here, as in the next sentence
ut...vix ratiō inīrī posset: *with the result that a plan/method* (ratiō) *was hardly able to be undertaken* (inīrī)
quō...currerētur aut cui...ferrētur: *as to where one might run first or to what situation help might be brought*; indirect questions with *ratiō inīrī*

5 Tamen, quod īnstitūtō Caesaris semper duae legiōnēs prō castrīs excubābant plūrēsque partītīs temporibus erant in opere, celeriter factum est ut aliī ēruptiōnibus resisterent, aliī turrēs redūcerent aggeremque interscinderent, omnis vērō ex castrīs multitūdō ad restinguendum concurreret.

ēruptiō, -iōnis f.: sudden rush of troops from a position; a sally
excubō (1): keep watch
īnstitūtum, īnstitūtī n.: design, plan, order; intention
interscindō, -ere, -ī, scissus: tear asunder, split
partiō, -īre, -īvī, -ītus: distribute
plūrēs, plūria: many
redūcō, -ere: (here) move back
resistō, -ere, -restitī: oppose, withstand (+ dat)
restinguō, -ere, -stinxī, -stinctus: extinguish, mitigate; exterminate
vērō: in fact; even; but indeed

5: see Appendix A for a basic diagram of this sentence; Caesar lists three outcomes, singling out two distinct groups and their tasks (*aliī...aliī*) and then the gaggle of soldiers in general (*omnis multitūdō*)
plūrēsque partītīs temporibus erant in opere: two legions kept watch at the ready (*excubāre*) while many others were busy with the construction
factum est ut: *it was quickly accomplished that*; *it was quickly seen to that*; impers.
turrēs redūcerent aggeremque interscinderent: some of the Roman soldiers are pulling back the siege towers to get them away from the hurled firebrands and the Gallic *cunīculī*, and are also digging in the *agger* to locate or destroy the *cunīculī*. *interscinderent* is a bit troublesome here: it would make no sense for the Romans to "tear asunder" their *agger* at this point. Caes. uses *interscindere* only one other time, of Gauls attempting to tear up a bridge (*BG* 2.9)
ad restinguendum: gerund construction expressing purpose

[25] *The Gauls continue to attack Roman constructions*

1 Cum in omnibus locīs cōnsūmptā iam relīquā parte noctis pugnārētur semperque hostibus spēs victōriae redintegrārētur, eō magis quod deustōs pluteōs turrium vidēbant nec facile adīre apertōs ad auxiliandum animadvertēbant, semperque ipsī recentēs dēfessīs succēderent omnemque Galliae salūtem in illō vestīgiō temporis positam arbitrārentur,

---

aperiō, -īre, -uī, -pertus: uncover, expose; explain, recount; reveal
arbitror, -ārī, -ātus: observe, consider; decide, judge
auxilior, -ārī, -ātus:: aid, assist
dēfessus, -a, -um: exhausted, tired
deūrō, -ere, -ussī, -ustus: burn down, consume
pluteus, -eī m.: covering, shed
recēns, -tis: recent, fresh, young
redintegrō (1): renew; revive
salūs, -tis f.: health; prosperity
spēs, -eī f.: hope
succēdō, -ere, -cessī, -cessus: follow, take the place of (+ dat)
vestigium, -ī n.: (of time) point, moment, instant; (elsewhere) a footprint, trace

---

Cum: an extended circumstantial clause which will not end until *arbitrārentur*; see Appendix A for a diagram of this sentence
eō magis quod: *the more so because*
nec facile adīre apertōs: *and that [our men], exposed, could not easily approach*
ipsī: the Gauls
in illō vestīgiō temporis positam: *rested on this very moment in time*

accidit īnspectantibus nōbīs quod, dignum memoriā vīsum, praetereundum nōn exīstimāvimus. 2 Quīdam ante portam oppidī Gallus per manūs sēbī ac picis trāditās glaebās in ignem ē regiōne turris prōiciēbat; scorpiōne ab latere dextrō trāiectus exanimātusque concidit.

---

concidō, -ere, -dī, —: fall, die
dexter, -tra, -trum: right-hand; skillful; favorable, fortunate
exanimō (1): kill; scare; exhaust
glaeba, -ae f.: lump, clod, glob
latus, lateris n.: side, flank
pix, picis f.: pitch, tar
praetereō, -īre, -īvī, -itus: pass by, disregard, omit, miss
prōiciō, -ere, -iēcī, -iectus: hurl, throw forth
quī-, quae-, quoddam: a certain, a certain one
sēbum, -ī n.: grease, tallow
trāiciō, -ere, -ēcī, -ectus: pierce, pierce; transport; break through

---

accidit...quod: *there happened... [something] which*
dignum memoriā vīsum: *having seemed [to Caes.] worthy of memory*
praetereundum nōn: sc. *esse* for the passive periphrastic infin. in ind. statement
per manūs...trāditās: *passed [to him] by hand*
scorpiōne: The *scorpiō* was a large torsion-powered projectile weapon which fired a bolt at extreme velocity. It was very accurate, could pierce armor and shields, and inflicted terrible carnage. Caesar sometimes refers to these weapons as *tormenta* (cf. *BG* 2.8.4; 4.25.1-2), which is a more general term for any device which is powered by twisting (*torquendō*) fibers, used also of cranes (7.22.2 above) and torture racks (*BG* 6.19.3). Though Caesar mentions the legionnaires' use of *pīla* (javelins) regularly, he rarely mentions other types of missile weapons in the legions, even though they must have been present; cf. *BG* 4.25.1, when he orders the Britons to be driven back by slings, arrows, and artillery: *fundīs, sagittīs, tormentīs hostēs propellī ac submovērī iussit*

3 Hunc ex proximīs ūnus iacentem trānsgressus eōdem illō mūnere fungēbātur; 4 eādem ratiōne ictū scorpiōnis exanimātō alterī successit tertius, et tertiō quārtus, nec prius ille est ā prōpugnātōribus vacuus relictus locus quam restinctō aggere atque omnī ex parte summōtīs hostibus fīnis est pugnandī factus.

---

fīnis, -is m. end, conclusion; boundary, territory
fungor, -ī, fūnctus: engage in, discharge, perform (+ abl)
iaceō, -ēre, -uī, —: lie, lie dead
ictus, -ūs m.: blow, stroke, wound
mūnus, -eris n.: duty, service; gift
prōpugnātor, -ōris m.: defender
restinguō, -ere, -stīnxī, -stinctus: extinguish; destroy; mitigate
succēdō, -ere, -cessī, -cessus: follow, take the place of (+ dat)
summoveō, -ēre, -mōvī, -mōtus: remove; drive off, dislodge; expel
trānsgredior, -ī, -gressus: cross, climb over, step over; desert
vacuus, -a, -um: empty, unoccupied, unmanned

---

ex proximīs ūnus: *one from the nearby [Gauls]*
mūnere: *duty;* abl. singular object of *fungēbātur*
exanimātō alterī: dative with *successit*
īctū: ablative of means
ille...locus: *this position*
prius...quam: *earlier...than, until*
fīnis est pugnandī factus: *an end was made of the fighting*; gerund

[26] *Women of the town take matters into their own hands*

1 Omnia expertī Gallī, quod rēs nūlla successerat, posterō diē cōnsilium cēpērunt ex oppidō profugere hortante et iubente Vercingetorīge. 2 Id silentiō noctis cōnātī nōn magnā iactūrā suōrum sēsē effectūrōs spērābant, propterea quod nēque longē ab oppidō castra Vercingetorīgis aberant, et palūs quae perpetua intercēdēbat Rōmānōs ad īnsequendum tardābat.

---

absum, -esse: be away/far from
cōnor, -ārī, -ātus: attempt, make an effort; exert oneself
efficiō, -ere, -fēcī, -fectus: cause, bring about; accomplish
experior, -īrī, -pertus: test, attempt; try
īnsequor, -ī, -cūtus: follow; attack
intercēdō, -ere, -cessī, -cessus: lie between; intervene
iactūra, -ae f.: loss, cost, damage
perpetuus, -a, -um: continuous
posterus, a, um: next, following
profūgiō, -ere, -gī, -gitus: escape, escape from; run away from
propterea: (with *quod*) because, with the view that
spērō (1): hope for; look forward to
succēdō, -ere, -cessī, -cessus: (here) turn out, succeed
tardō (1): check; hinder, slow

---

quod rēs nūlla successerat: *because no attempt [of theirs] had succeeded*
cōnsilium cēpērunt: *made a plan*
hortante et iubente Vercingetorīge: abl. abs.; the order perhaps suggests that Verc. at first suggested, and then ultimately ordered them to withdraw
cōnātī: *having attempted*

3 Iamque hoc facere noctū apparābant cum mātrēs familiae repente in pūblicum prōcurrērunt flentēsque prōiectae ad pedēs suōrum omnibus precibus petiērunt nē sē et commūnēs līberōs hostibus ad supplicium dēderent quōs ad capiendam fugam nātūrae et vīrium īnfirmitās impedīret.

---

apparō (1): prepare, equip, provide; attempt; organize
commūnis, -e: in common, shared
dēdō, -ere, -didī, -ditus: give up, surrender; abandon; hand over
fleō, -ēre, -ēvī, -ētus: cry, weep
īnfirmitās, -tātis f.: weakness
līberī, -ōrum m.: children
prex, precis f.: prayer, request
prōcurrō, -ere, -currī, -cursus: run out, rush forward, charge
prōiciō, -ere, -iēcī, -iectus: hurl, throw forth; cast out; abandon
repente: suddenly; unexpectedly
supplicium, -iī n.: punishment

---

hoc facere: *to do this* (depart from the town)
mātrēs familiae: Caesar infrequently mentions women in *Gallic Wars* and even more infrequently do they have any agency; he will again note the actions of women during a siege at *BG* 7.47.4-6. Typically the terms Caesar uses are *mulierēs, uxōrēs,* or *mātrēs familiae*, as here. For women in the *Gallic Wars* see Jane Bellemore, "Caesar's Gallic Women under Siege," *Latomus* 2016: 888-902
ad supplicium dēderent: *abandon to punishment/torture/suffering*
quōs…īnfirmitās impedīret: *whom weakness was hindering from* (+ *ad*)
vīrium: gen. pl. of irregular noun *vīs*, in the plural meaning "physical strength"

4 Ubi eōs in sententiā perstāre vīdērunt, quod plērumque in summō perīculō timor misericordiam nōn recipit, conclāmāre et significāre dē fugā Rōmānīs coepērunt.
5 Quō timōre perterritī Gallī, nē ab equitātū Rōmānōrum viae praeoccupārentur, cōnsiliō dēstitērunt.

---

conclāmō (1): cry, shout aloud; signal
dēsistō, -ere, -stitī, -titus: cease, leave off, give over
misericordia, -ae f.: pity, mercy
perstō, -āre, -titī, -stātus: persist, stand firmly, remain unmoved
plērumque: mostly, generally
praeoccupō (1): seize; anticipate
sententia, -ae, f.: way of thinking, judgment, opinion; decision, intent
significō (1): indicate, show

---

eōs in sententiā perstāre: *that [the men] stood firmly in their opinion*
nē...viae...praeoccupārentur: *[fearing] that the routes be seized*

[27] *Caesar's forces take the wall*

1 Posterō diē Caesar prōmōtā turrī perfectīsque operibus quae facere īnstituerat, magnō coortō imbre nōn inūtilem hanc ad capiendum cōnsilium tempestātem arbitrātus est, quod paulō incautius cūstōdiās in mūrō dispositās vidēbat, suōsque languidius in opere versārī iussit et quid fierī vellet ostendit.

---

coorior, -īrī, -ortus: appear, originate; arise, break out; be born
cūstōdia, -ae f.: guard; protection
dispōnō, -ere, -posuī, -positus: place, distribute; arrange, lay out
imber, imbris m.: rain, storm
incautus, -a, -um: careless
inūtilis, -e: useless, unprofitable, inexpedient, disadvantageous
languidē: lazily, slowly; listlessly
perficiō, -ere, -fēcī, -fectus: finish, accomplish
posterus, a, um: next, following
prōmoveō, -ēre, -mōvī, -mōtus: move forward, advance; increase
tempestās, -tātis f.: weather, storm; season, time
versō (1): (in pass.) be occupied with, situated in; remain in; (in act.) turn, upturn, revolve

---

1: see Appendix A for a diagram of this sentence
turrī: abl. sing. fem. (i-stem) with *prōmōtā* in abl. abs.
operibus perfectīs: abl. abs.; *operibus* is antecedent of the following relative clause
inutilem: sc. *esse;* pred. adj. after *arbitrātus est*
ad capiendum cōnsilium: *for the execution of a plan*; gerundive
suōsque: the *-que* connects the two main clauses *arbitrātus est* and *iussit et...ostendit*;
quid fierī vellet: *what he wished to be done*

2 Legiōnibusque intrā vīneās in occultō expedītīs, cohortātus ut aliquandō prō tantīs labōribus frūctum victōriae perciperent; eīs quī prīmī mūrum ascendissent praemia prōposuit mīlitibusque signum dedit. 3 Illī subitō ex omnibus partibus ēvolāvērunt mūrumque celeriter complēvērunt.

---

aliquandō: for once, now; at last
ascendō, -ere, -ī, -cēnsus: climb; mount, scale
compleō, -ēre, -ēvī, -ētus: fill up; occupy, crowd
ēvolō (1): rush out, forth; fly
expediō, -īre, -īvī, -ītus: settle, arrange; let loose; bring forward
frūctus, -ūs m.: produce, fruit
occultus, -a, -um: hidden, secret
percipiō, -ere, -cēpī, -ceptus: seize wholly, take; harvest
praemium, -iī n.: reward
prīmus, -a, -um: first, early
prōpōnō, -ere, -posuī, -positus: lay out; declare; offer
subitō: suddenly, unexpectedly
vīnea, -ae f.: covering, shelter, makeshift roof

---

intrā vīneās: the text here is disputed, with some manuscripts showing *extrā vīneās* or even *extrā castra intrā vīneās*; the sense seems clear: that the legionnaires are somehow using the Roman siege "sheds" to move forward in sufficient numbers to make a difference, and without the Gauls noticing in the rainy weather

ut aliquandō...frūctum: Here Caesar indulges in a rare moment of literary playfulness by making a pun on the *vīneae* as protective structures (see 7.17.1) and the more common meaning of humble grape trellises, for which the defensive contraptions were no doubt named. He thus asks the soldiers to pluck the *frūctum victōriae* owed to them *prō tantīs labōribus*. *aliquandō* is also colloquial, perhaps a joke on their lack of success in this siege until this point

quī primī...ascendissent: *who will have been first to climb*; in ind. st., the fut. pf. indic. becomes plupf. subj. after a a past main verb (*Bradley's Arnold* §524 n.2)

[28] *The Roman soldiers massacre the inhabitants of Avaricum*

1 Hostēs rē novā perterritī mūrō turribusque dēiectī in forō ac locīs patentiōribus cuneātim cōnstitērunt, hōc animō ut sī quā ex parte contrā venīrētur aciē īnstrūctā dēpugnārent.

---

aciēs, -eī, f.: battle line, formation
cōnstō (1): stand together; stand firm; agree, fit; be based upon; exist
cuneātim: in a closely packed wedge; wedge-shaped
dēiciō, -ere, -iēcī, -iectus: throw, toss down from; cause to fall
dēpugnō (1): fight hard, do battle
īnstruō, -ere, -strūxī, -strūctus: draw up; construct; prepare; fit out
novus, -a, um: new; strange
patēns, -entis: open, accessible

---

rē novā perterritī mūrō turribusque dēiectī: *having been terrified by this new circumstance and having been thrown from the wall and towers*; the Gauls flee the walls at the sight of the siege towers, uncharacteristically timid behavior perhaps justified by the storm or the feats of Roman engineering; cf. 2.12, 2.30, 3.21
cuneātim: the adverb appears only here and once in Apuleius *Met.* (8.15.35); the root **cunea-* pertains to a wedge shape, with an adjective (*cuneatus* "pointed like a wedge"), a verb (*cuneāre* "secure with wedges") and a noun (*cuneus* "wedge shape")
hōc animō ut: *with the following intention, that…*
venīrētur: *if [an attack] were to come*, lit. "if there were an arrival"
aciē īnstrūctā: rather than panicking, the Gauls have chosen a relatively open area within the walls to make a desperate last stand in an ordered defensive formation

2 Ubi nēminem in aequum locum sēsē dēmittere, sed tōtō undique mūrō circumfundī vīdērunt, veritī nē omnīnō spēs fugae tollerētur, abiectīs armīs ultimās oppidī partēs continentī impetū petīvērunt, 3 parsque ibi cum angustō exitū portārum sē ipsī premerent ā mīlitibus, pars iam ēgressa portīs ab equitibus est interfecta; 4 nec fuit quisquam quī praedae studēret.

---

abiciō, -ere, -iēci, -iēctus: throw away, cast aside; abandon
aequus, -a, -um: level; favorable
angustus, -a, -um: narrow, close
circumfundō, -ere, -fūdī, -fūsus: pour/crowd around; surround
continēns, -ntis: continual
dēmittō, -ere, dēmīsī, demissus: drop, let fall; sink; send/cast down
impetus, -ūs m.: attack; (here) rush
nēmō, nullīus m./f.: no one
omnīnō: entirely, altogether
praeda, -ae f.: booty, loot, spoils
spēs, -eī, f.: hope
tollō, -ere, sustulī, sublātus: raise up, elevate; remove, abolish, ruin
undique: from every direction, place, source; on both sides
vereor, -ērī, -itus: fear; respect

2-4: see Appendix A for a diagram of this sentence
nēminem: anticipates a corresponding [*omnēs*] as subject of *circumfundī*
in aequum locum sēsē dēmittere: the Romans have poured onto the top of the wall from their *turrēs*, and now the Gauls expect them to descend the inner side into the inner area (*aequum locum*) of the town
veritī nē...tollerētur: fear clause
quisquam: sc. *Rōmānus*; the perspective shifts from Gauls to Romans here
studēret: *was focusing attention to;* + dat; the Roman soldiers are in no mood to be distracted by plundering or taking slaves, but instead are focused on killing. See Appendix C for a brief discussion of Roman sacking of cities

Sīc et Cenabī caede et labōre operis incitātī nōn aetāte
cōnfectīs, nōn mulieribus, nōn īnfantibus pepercērunt.
5 Dēnique ex omnī numerō quī fuit circiter mīlium XL, vix
DCCC, quī prīmō clāmōre audītō sē ex oppidō ēiēcērunt,
incolumēs ad Vercingetorīgem pervēnērunt, quōs ille multā
iam nocte silentiō ex fugā excēpit.

---

aetās, -tātis f.: age, lifetime
caedis, -is f.: murder, massacre
circiter: approximately, about
confectus, -a, -um: impaired, reduced, weakened
dēnique: finally, in the end
ēiciō, -ere, ēiēcī, ēiectus: cast out, fling up expel; discharge, vomit
excipiō, -ere, excēpī, exceptus: take out; remove; follow
incitō (1): hasten, arouse, agitate
incolumis, -e: unharmed, uninjured; alive, safe; unimpaired
īnfāns, -antis m./f.: infant; child
parcō, -ere, pepercī, parsus: spare, show consideration to (+ dat)
vix: hardly, scarcely, barely

Cenabī: *of/at Cenabum,* the place where Roman merchants had been massacred early in the crisis (see *BG* 7.3.1)
aetāte cōnfectīs: *(those) having been impaired by age*; the PPP of the verb *cōnficere*, which can sometimes mean "weaken, reduce, destroy"
ad Vercingetorīgem: to his *castra* and/or forces
multā iam nocte: *late at night;* idiomatic, abl. of time when
silentiō ex fugā excēpit: *removed from their flight in silence*; the subject is Verc.

6 Veritus nē qua in castrīs ex eōrum concursū et misericordiā vulgī sēditiō orerētur, ut procul in viā dispositīs familiāribus suīs principibusque cīvitātum disparandōs dēdūcendōsque ad suōs cūrāret quae cuique cīvitātī pars castrōrum ab initiō obvēnerat.

---

concursus, -ūs m.: tumult, confusion; collision; crowd
dēdūcō, -ere, -dūxi, -ductus: lead away, divert; conduct; withdraw
disparō (1): separate, divide
dispōnō, -ere, -posuī, -positus: dispose, distribute; manage; appoint, post, station
familiāris, -e.: familiar, intimate, friendly
misericordia, -ae f.: pity, sympathy; compassion, mercy
obveniō, -īre, -ī, -tus: be allotted; meet, come before, come against
orior, -īrī/-ī, -tus: rise; emerge
procul: at a distance
sēditiō, -iōnis f.: discord, strife
vereor, -ērī, -itus: fear; respect
vulgus, -ī m.: the people, masses

Veritus: s.c *est*; the subject is Vercingetorix; introduces a fear clause. See Appendix A for a diagram of this complicated final sentence
qua…concursū et misericordiā…sēditiō: *some strife…from the tumult and the sympathy…*; the two causes of potential *sēditiō*, arranged in *hendiadys*
procul: specifically, far away in advance of the camp
dispositīs: *having been placed* (stationed by Vercingetorix); abl. absolute
disparandōs dēdūcendōsque: *(he made sure) that (those [refugees]) must be separated and led away;* passive periphrastic infinitives in ind. st. after *cūrāret*
quae cuique cīvitātī pars: rewrite the sentence as if: *[eōs] disparandōs…in eam partem castrōrum quae obvēnerat cuique cīvitātī ab initiō*; i.e., "[the refugees] must be diverted into that part of the camp which had been allotted to each faction/tribe from the outset"

APPENDIX A
Supplemental Sentence Diagrams

7.2.1-2

Hīs rēbus agitātīs profitentur Carnūtēs sē nūllum perīculum commūnis salūtis causā recūsāre prīncipēsque ex omnibus bellum factūrōs pollicentur et, quoniam in praesentiā obsidibus cavēre inter sē nōn possint nē rēs efferātur, ut iūreiūrandō ac fidē sanciātur petunt, collātīs mīlitāribus signīs (quō mōre eōrum gravissima caerimōnia continētur), nē factō initiō bellī ab reliquīs dēserantur.

Carnūtēs

profitentur (that) sē nūllum perīculum recūsāre

pollicentur (that) [sē prīncipēs] bellum factūrōs [esse]

petunt ut iūreiūrandō ac fidē sanciātur

nē ab reliquīs dēserantur

quoniam nōn possint cavēre obsidibus inter sē

nē rēs efferātur

7.5.6

Id eāne dē causā quam lēgātīs prōnūntiārunt, an perfidiā adductī fēcerint, quod nihil nōbīs cōnstat, nōn vidētur prō certō esse prōpōnendum.

nōn vidētur (that) [my judgment] prō certō esse prōpōnendum

quod nihil nōbis cōnstat

(whether): [fēcerint] id dē causā (quam lēgātīs prōnūntiā[vē]runt)

(or): fēcerint adductī perfidiā

7.10.1

…sī reliquam partem hiemis ūnō locō legiōnēs continēret, nē stīpendiāriīs Aeduōrum expugnātīs cūncta Gallia dēficeret, quod nūllum amīcīs in eō praesidium vidērētur positum esse; sī mātūrius ex hībernīs ēdūceret, nē ab rē frūmentāriā dūrīs subvectiōnibus labōrāret.

sī [Caesar] continēret legiōnēs ūnō locō

[there was a fear] nē cūncta Gallia dēficeret (stīpendiāriīs expugnātīs)

quod vidērētur (that) nūllum praesidium positum esse

sī ēdūceret [legiōnēs] ex hībernīs mātūrius

[there was a fear] nē labōrāret (dūrīs subvectiōnibus)

7.13.2

Eōrum impetum Gallī sustinēre nōn potuērunt atque in fugam coniectī multīs āmissīs sē ad agmen recēpērunt. Quibus prōflīgātīs rūrsus oppidānī perterritī comprehensōs eōs, quōrum operā plēbem concitātam exīstimābant, ad Caesarem perdūxērunt sēsēque eī dēdidērunt.

Gallī nōn potuērunt sustinēre impetum

atque [Gallī] recēpērunt sē ad agmen.

coniectī in fugam (multīs āmissīs)

Oppidānī perterritī

perdūxērunt eōs comprehensōs ad Caesarem

quōrum operā exīstimābant (that) plēbem concitātam [esse]

(and) dēdidērunt sēsē (to Caesar)

7.15.4-5

Prōcumbunt omnibus Gallīs ad pedēs Biturigēs nē pulcherrimam prope tōtīus Galliae urbem, quae praesidiō et ōrnāmentō sit cīvitātī, suīs manibus succendere cōgerentur; facile sē locī nātūrā dēfēnsūrōs dīcunt quod prope ex omnibus partibus flūmine et palūde circumdatā ūnum habeat et perangustum aditum.

Biturigēs (1) prōcumbunt

[begging] nē urbem suīs manibus succendere cōgerentur

quae sit praesidiō et ōrnāmentō (for) cīvitātī;

(2) dīcunt (that) sē facile dēfēnsūrōs [esse] [urbem]

quod [urbs] habeat ūnum et perangustum aditum

(flūmine et palūde circumdatā)

7.17.2

Dē rē frūmentāriā Boiōs atque Aeduōs adhortārī nōn dēstitit; quōrum alterī, quod nūllō studiō agēbant, nōn multum adiuvābant, alterī nōn magnīs facultātibus, quod cīvitās erat exigua et īnfirma, celeriter quod habuērunt cōnsūmpsērunt.

nōn dēstitit adhortārī Boiōs atque Aeduōs dē rē frūmentāriā;

alterī quōrum (the Aedui) nōn multum adiuvābant

quod nūllō studiō agēbant

alterī [quōrum](the Boii) celeriter [the food] cōnsūmpsērunt

quod habuērunt

quod cīvitās erat exigua et īnfirma

(nōn magnīs facultātibus)

7.17.3

Summā difficultāte reī frumentāriae adfectō exercitū tenuitāte Boiōrum, indīligentiā Aeduōrum, incendiīs aedificiōrum, usque eō ut complūrēs diēs frūmentō mīlitēs caruerint et pecore ex longinquiōribus vīcīs adāctō extrēmam famem sustentārent, nūlla tamen vōx est ab eīs audīta populī Rōmānī maiestāte et superiōribus victōriīs indigna.

(although) exercitū adfectō (by the) summā difficultāte

(due to) (a) tenuitāte Boiōrum

(b) indīligentiā Aeduōrum

(c) incendiīs aedificiōrum

usque eō ut mīlitēs

caruerint frūmento

sustentārent extrēmam famem (pecore adāctō)

tamen nūlla vox audīta [est] ab eis [mīlitibus]

[quae sit] indigna maiestāte et victōriīs

7.18.1

Cum iam mūrō turrēs appropinquāssent, ex captīvīs Caesar cognōvit Vercingetorīgem cōnsūmptō pābulō castra mōvisse propius Avāricum atque ipsum cum equitātū expedītīsque, quī inter equitēs proeliārī cōnsuēssent, īnsidiārum causā eō prōfectum quō nostrōs posterō diē pābulātum ventūrōs arbitrārētur.

Caesar cognōvit (that) (cōnsūmptō pābulō)

cum iam mūrō turrēs appropinquā[vi]ssent

(a) Vercingetorīgem mōvisse castra

(b) (Verc.) ipsum prōfectum [esse]

cum equitātū expedītīsque

quī cōnsuē[vi]ssent proeliārī

eō → quō arbitrārētur (that) nostros ventūrōs [esse]

7.19.2-3

Hōc sē colle, interruptīs pontibus, Gallī fīdūciā locī continēbant, generātimque distribūtī in cīvitātēs, omnia vada ac saltūs eius palūdīs obtinēbant, sīc animō parātī, ut, sī eam palūdem Rōmānī perrumpere cōnārentur, haesitantēs premerent ex locō superiōre, ut quī propinquitātem locī vidēret parātōs prope aequō Mārte ad dīmicandum exīstimāret, quī inīquitātem condiciōnis perspiceret inānī simulātiōne sēsē ostentāre cognōsceret.

(interruptīs pontibus)

Gallī (a) continēbant sē [in] hōc colle fīdūciā locī

(b) obtinēbant omnia vada ac saltūs eius palūdis

distribūtī generātim in cīvitātēs

parātī sīc animō

ut[1] (sī Rōmānī perrumpere cōnārentur), premerent [eōs] haesitantēs

ut[2] [a person] existimāret (quī vidēret propinquitātem locī)

(that) [eōs] parātōs [esse] ad dīmicandum

[a person] cognōsceret (quī perspiceret inīquitātem condiciōnis)

(that) sēsē ostentāre inānī simulātiōne

---

1 "so prepared in their hearts that…" (result)
2 "with the general result that" (result)

7.19.4–5

Indignantēs mīlitēs Caesar, quod cōnspectum suum hostēs perferre possent tantulō spatiō interiectō, et signum proelī exposcentēs ēdocet, quantō dētrīmentō et quot virōrum fortium morte necesse sit cōnstāre victōriam; quōs cum sīc animō parātōs videat ut nūllum prō suā laude perīculum recūsent, summae sē inīquitātis condemnārī dēbēre nisi eōrum vītam suā salūte habeat cāriōrem.

Caesar ēdocet mīlites
indignantēs (quod hostēs possent perferre cōnspectum suum)
exposcentēs signum proelī
(that) necesse sit (that) victoriam cōnstāre
(a) quantō dētrīmentō
(b) quot virōrum fortium morte;

(and that) sē dēbēre condemnārī summae inīquitātis
cum videat (that) quōs sīc parātos [esse]
ut recūsent nūllum perīculum
nisi habeat vītam eōrum [esse] cāriōrem suā salūte

7.20.1-2

Vercingetorīx, cum ad suōs redīsset, prōditiōnis īnsimulātus, quod castra propius Rōmānōs mōvisset, quod cum omnī equitātū discessisset, quod sine imperiō tantās cōpiās relīquisset, quod eius discessū Rōmānī tantā opportūnitāte et celeritāte vēnissent; nōn haec omnia fortuitō aut sine cōnsiliō accidere potuisse; rēgnum illum Galliae mālle Caesaris concessū quam ipsōrum habēre beneficiō.

Verc. īnsimulātus [est] prōditiōnis (cum ad suōs redisset)

(a) quod mōvisset castra propius Rōmānōs

(b) quod discessissest cum omnī equitātū

(c) quod relīquisset tantās cōpiās sine imperiō

(d) quod (by means of his) discessū Rōmānī vēnissent

[the Gauls further add that]

(a) haec omnia nōn potuisse accidere fortuitō aut sine cōnsiliō

(b) illum (Verc.) mālle habēre rēgnum Galliae concessū Caesaris

quam (rather than) beneficiō [Gallōrum] ipsōrum

7.20.5

summam imperiī sē cōnsultō nūllī discēdentem trādidisse nē is multitūdinis studiō ad dīmicandum impellerētur, cui reī propter animī mollitiem studēre omnēs vidēret, quod diūtius labōrem ferre nōn possent[.]

[Verc.] respondit (that) sē cōnsultō trādidisse summam imperiī nūllī

nē is impellerētur ad dīmicandum studiō multitūdinis

cuī reī[3] [Verc.] vidēret (that) omnēs studēre

(quod [mīlitēs Gallicī] nōn possent ferre labōrem diūtius)

---

[3] to which end (i.e., the *studium* of the Gauls *ad dīmicandum*)

7.20.6

Rōmānī sī cāsū intervēnerint, fortūnae, sī alicuius indiciō vocātī, huic habendam grātiam, quod et paucitātem eōrum ex locō superiōre cognōscere et virtūtem dēspicere potuerint quī dīmicāre nōn ausī turpiter sē in castra recēperint.

[Verc. says that] grātiam fortūnae habendam [esse]
sī Rōmānī cāsū intervēnerint
[gratiam] huic [habendam esse]
sī [Rōmānī] indiciō alicuius vocātī sint
quod [Gallī] potuerint
et cognōscere paucitātem eōrum
et dēspicere virtūtem [eōrum]
quī sē in castra recēperint
nōn ausī dīmicāre turpiter

7.24.5

Tamen, quod īnstitūtō Caesaris semper duae legiōnēs prō castrīs excubābant plūrēsque partītīs temporibus erant in opere, celeriter factum est ut aliī ēruptiōnibus resisterent, aliī turrēs redūcerent aggeremque interscinderent, omnis vērō ex castrīs multitūdō ad restinguendum concurreret.

Tamen, quod semper (īnstitūtō Caesaris) (a) duae legiōnēs excubābant
(b) plūrēs erant in opere

celeriter factum est ut:

(a) aliī ēruptiōnibus resisterent

(b) aliī redūcerent turrēs [et] aggerem interscinderent

(c) omnis multitūdō concurreret ad restinguendum

7.25.1

Cum in omnibus locīs cōnsūmptā iam relīquā parte noctis pugnārētur semperque hostibus spēs victōriae redintegrārētur, eō magis quod deustōs pluteōs turrium vidēbant nec facile adīre apertōs ad auxiliandum animadvertēbant, semperque ipsī recentēs dēfessīs succēderent omnemque Galliae salūtem in illō vestīgiō temporis positam arbitrārentur, accidit īnspectantibus nōbīs quod, dignum memoriā vīsum, praetereundum nōn exīstimāvimus.

Cum (iam relīquā parte noctis cōnsūmptā)
(a) pugnārētur in omnibus locīs
(b) spēs victōriae semper redintegrārētur hostibus
eō magis quod
(a) vidēbant (that) pluteōs turrium deustōs [esse]
(b) animadvertēbant (that) nec facile [nostrōs] adīre
(c) semperque ipsī [Gallī] succēderent recentēs dēfessīs
(d) arbitrārentur (that) salutem Galliae positam [esse]
accidit īnspectantibus nōbīs [an event] dignum memoriā vīsum
quod praetereundum [esse] nōn exīstimāvimus

7.27.1

Posterō diē Caesar prōmōtā turrī perfectīsque operibus quae facere īnstituerat, magnō coortō imbre nōn inūtilem hanc ad capiendum cōnsilium tempestātem arbitrātus est, quod paulō incautius cūstōdiās in mūrō dispositās vidēbat, suōsque languidius in opere versārī iussit et quid fierī vellet ostendit.

(posterō diē)(turrī prōmōta)(operibus perfectīs)

quae facere īnstituerat

(magnō imbre coortō)

Caesar (a) arbitrātus est (that) hanc tempestātem [esse] nōn inūtilem

quod vidēbat (that) cūstōdiās dispositās [esse] paulō incautius

(b) iussit suōs [mīlitēs] versārī in opere languidius

(c) ostendit quid vellet fierī

7.28.2-4

Ubi nēminem in aequum locum sēsē dēmittere, sed tōtō undique mūrō circumfundī vīdērunt, veritī nē omnīnō spēs fugae tollerētur, abiectīs armīs ultimās oppidī partēs continentī impetū petīvērunt, parsque ibi cum angustō exitū portārum sē ipsī premerent ā mīlitibus, pars iam ēgressa portīs ab equitibus est interfecta;

Ubi [hostēs] vīdērunt (that) nēminem [Rōmānōrum] dēmittere sēsē

sed (that) [omnēs Rōmānōs] circumfundī mūrō tōtō

[hostēs] (armīs abiectīs) petīvērunt partēs ultimās oppidī

parsque interfecta [est] ā mīlitibus

cum ipsī premerent sē angustō exitū portārum

[et] pars [interfecta est] ab equitibus

ēgressa iam portīs

7.28.6

Veritus nē qua in castrīs ex eōrum concursū et misericordiā vulgī sēditiō orerētur, ut procul in viā dispositīs familiāribus suīs prīncipibusque cīvitātum disparandōs dēdūcendōsque ad suōs cūrāret, quae cuique cīvitātī pars castrōrum ab initiō obvēnerat.

[Verc.] veritus [est]

nē qua sēditiō orerētur ex eōrum concursū et misericordiā vulgī

ut [Verc.] cūrāret (that) [eōs (fugientēs)]

disparandōs dēdūcendōsque [esse]

[in] par[tem castrōrum]

quae obvēnerat cuique cīvitātī

APPENDIX B
Proper Nouns in the Text

Aedui (5, 9, 10, 17)(also Haedui): A powerful tribe situated in modern Burgundy, between the Saône and Loire rivers. They were reluctant allies of the Romans throughout the first six years of the war. Caesar sometimes used their chief *oppidum* (Bibracte, at Mont Beuvray) as a central depot and fortress.

Arverni (4, 5, 7, 8): A powerful tribe situated in the modern Auvergne region. In the 3rd and 2nd centuries BCE they had enjoyed a general hegemony over Gaul from the Atlantic to the Rhine, but were defeated by the Romans in 121 BCE, after which their influence was reduced. By the time of the events of *Gallic War*, there were two main *factiōnēs* in Gaul: the Aedui were the unofficial leaders of one, and the Arverni the other (*BG* 1.31). Their chief *oppidum* was Gergovia, near modern Clermont-Ferrand.

Avaricum (12, 15, 16): The chief *oppidum* of the Bituriges, near Bourges.

Boii (9, 10, 17): The tribe mentioned by Caesar here in Book VII are a mere fraction of a much larger group of Gauls under the name, first seen in history in 390 BCE when they took part in the Gallic invasion of Italy. Caesar had defeated the sub-group mentioned here along with the Helvetii back in 58, and had installed the survivors as dependents of the Aedui at the *oppidum* Gergobinna (location unknown).

Bituriges (5, 8, 9, 11, 12, 13, 15, 21): A tribe of central Gaul. Their chief *oppidum* was Avaricum.

Carnutes (2, 11): A tribe which inhabited a large territory between the Seine and the Loire. Their chief *oppida* were at Cenabum (Orléans) and Autricum (Chartres).

Cenabum (3, 4, 11, 14, 17, 28): The chief *oppidum* of the Carnutes, modern Orléans.

Gauls: A group of Celtic-speaking peoples of western and central Europe. The Gauls of Caesar's time were in their *La Tène* cultural epoch, which began about 450 BCE and stretched over what is now France, Belgium, and Switzerland. The boundaries of the territory were approximately defined by the Roman province of *Gallia Trānsalpīna* in the south (modern Provence) and the Rhine river in the northeast. The *La Tène* Gallic tribes were increasingly urbanized by the middle of the 1st century BCE, and many had established one or more *oppida* within their territories. The Gauls had a long history of contact with the Romans. In the 4th century BCE Gallic tribes crossed the Alps and settled the rich farmlands of the Po river in northern Italy, and in 390 BCE they famously sacked Rome (see *Senones*). Gallic forces fought with the Carthiginians against Rome in the Punic Wars, most notably with Hannibal's army at Cannae. Roman intervention in Gallic territory intensified in the mid to late 2nd century BCE, resulting in the successive defeats of the Arverni and the Allobroges and the creation of the Roman province stretching from the maritime Alps to the Pyrannees via the city of Narbo. Caesar's arrival in 58 and the events of his subsequent campaigns led to the ultimate incorporation of Gaul as a Roman province.

Gergovia (4): The chief *oppidum* of the Arverni, near modern Clermont-Ferrand.

Helvii (7, 8): A smaller tribe dwelling around the source of the Loire river, to the west of the Rhône. Their territory had been reduced by Pompey due to their support of Sertorius, but by the time of the *Gallic War* they were friendly to the Romans and, though outside the boundaries of Roman *Gallia Trānsalpīna*, were under Roman protection.

Lemovices (4): A smaller tribe dwelling around the modern district of Limousin. Their territory was rich in iron, tin, and gold. Their chief *oppidum* in Caesar's time was Durotincum (probably modern Villejoubert), but after their incorporation into Roman Aquitania the major town became Augustoritum (Limoges).

Liger (5, 11): The modern Loire river, originating in the mountains of the Massif Central in the territory of the Helvii. It flows north into Central Gaul between the lands of the Arverni and Aedui, then turns west through the territory of the Carnutes and Andes, reaching the Atlantic at Condevincum (modern Nantes), an *oppidum* of the Namnetes.

Lucterius (5, 7, 8): a leader of the Cadurci, a tribe of southwestern Gaul. He was a lieutenant of Vercingetorix and would continue to resist the Romans after Alesia. He was eventually captured by the Romans (*BG* 8.44).

Senones (4, 11): A tribe of central Gaul. A group bearing the same name, probably related, had led the invasion of Italy and defeated the Romans at the battle of the Allia in 390 BCE, after which they sacked Rome. They then settled in northern Italy and remained there until ousted by the Romans in 283. It is not known what became of them in the centuries after this. By the time of Caesar's *Gallic War*, the tribe he calls the Senones are dwelling in the Seine basin south and east of modern Paris.

These Senones had a long history of resistance to Caesar, and had most recently incurred his wrath back in the spring of 53. After defeating them Caesar stationed six legions in their winter camps within Senones territory (see 7.10). Their chief *oppida* were Agedincum (modern Sens) and Vellaunodunum (location unknown).

Trebonius, Gaius (11): quaestor in 60, tribune of the plebs in 55, by which time he was a supporter of the triumvirs. His *lex Trebonia* of that year secured five-year commands for Pompey in the two Spains and Crassus in Syria. As reward, Caesar took him as legate to Gaul. He led three legions in the second invasion of Britain in 54, and while wintering with one legion among the Belgae, he joined Caesar in aiding the besieged Q. Cicero. He besieged Massilia for Caesar during the Civil War, but would be a participant in his assassination in 44.

Vellaunodunum (11, 14): One of the *oppida* of the Senones. Its modern location is unknown.

Volcae Arecomici (7): A Gallic tribe which, by the time of *Gallic War*, was dwelling within the confines of the Roman province *Gallia Trānsalpīna*. Their chief *oppidum* was a very ancient site atop which the Romans would later found the veteran colony Nemausus (Nîmes).

APPENDIX C

The Roman Sacking of Cities

The standard verb used to refer to the Roman destruction of a city by the Augustan era was *dīripere*, "lay waste, plunder, pillage; snatch away," an event common enough that authors such as Livy felt little need to elaborate beyond providing that one word. Caesar's description of the sack of Avaricum is quite unusual in that regard, as he not only dedicates roughly half a chapter to its minutiae, but chooses not once to describe it as a *dīreptiō*, or indeed any related term. This would seem to be a conscious choice. But if not a *dīreptiō*, then how, exactly, does Caesar wish us to interpret his narrative of events at Avaricum, where Roman soldiers purportedly massacred some 40,000 Gallic men, women, and children?[1]

The archetypical Roman plundering described by Roman historians such as Livy or Tacitus[2] was predicated on a Roman commander turning their soldiers loose, giving the town's inhabitants and treasures to them, or in some other way refusing to assert form and authority over their army. Setting aside the much earlier, and less corroborated, "Polybian" model investigated by Ziolkowski,[3] the sacking of a town by Romans involved the army dissolving into individual soldiers and the city

---

[1] The massacre at Avaricum is just one piece of evidence in a larger discussion: did Caesar commit genocide in Gaul? See Raaflaub, "Caesar and Genocide: Confronting the Dark Side of Caesar's *Gallic Wars*," *New England Classical Journal* 48:1 (2021): 54-80; doi.org/10.52284/NECJ/48.1/article/raaflaub

[2] See, e.g., Tacitus *Histories* 3.33.1-3

[3] Adam Ziolkowski, "*Urbs direpta,* or how the Romans sacked cities" in *War and Society in the Roman World,* ed. J. Rich and G. Shipley (London/New York: Routledge, 1993/2002), 69-91

dissolving into countless individual objects of plunder. The first major break with this model made by Caesar's account of Avaricum, then, is "*parsque ibi cum angustō exitū portārum sē ipsī premerent ā mīlitibus, pars iam ēgressa portīs ab equitibus est interfecta*" ("some [of the Gauls], when they were pressing themselves there in the narrow opening of the gates, were killed by the [Roman] soldiers; others, now having emerged from the gates, were killed by the cavalry" 7.28.3). The use of synchysis[4] serves to reinforce the order with which the massacre was carried out by the coordinated maneuvers of infantry and cavalry: the massacre does not seem to be the work of a mob of uncontrolled marauders, but instead a precise military deployment designed to ensure the death of as many Gallic citizens as possible. Caesar seems to report this fact with pride as its orchestrator: he maintained control over his army in a situation where many other generals had not, and channeled them into as efficient an instrument of revenge as possible. Caesar describes a similarly vengeful act at *BG* 1.12.3-7, when his legions fall upon a group of Helvetii who, he explains, had humiliated a Roman army decades earlier.

The theme of systematic, focused destruction is reiterated in the other key difference between the sack of Avaricum and the typical Roman pillaging which Ziolkowski highlights in contemporary sources. The key phrase is "*nec fuit quisquam quī praedae studēret.*" ("nor was there any [Roman soldier] who focused their attention on looting" 7.28.4), with the hyperbole of *quisquam* and the relative clause of characteristic reiterating Caesar's pride in the accomplishment. The verb *studēret* carries weight, because here Caesar's forces are attentive in their violence. Soldiers who leave a city *dīrepta* metaphorically snatch it away, removing its valuables and inhabitants. By contrast, Caesar's soldiers neither took Avaricum with them nor left any of it behind. By implication, the fervor of vengeance for Cenabum seems to be so intense that plundering the city is

---

[4] a pattern of interlocking or deliberately confused word order

considered too kind a fate, because the goods and people associated with it would survive and so the legacy of the city would remain. Avaricum should not be considered unusual for its savagery or destruction, but for the focus and control which Caesar claims he and the army exercised over the carnage. The soldiers of his legions, he seems to suggest, possess exemplary *studium.*

Avaricum is elsewhere described as the jewel of the Bituriges (7.15.3–5), a strategic stronghold in central Gaul but not directly connected to the slaying of Romans by the Carnutes at Cenabum. Thus it is curious that Caesar describes the destruction of Avaricum as such a symbolically loaded act. Avaricum is the fourth town Caesar attacks in the nascent campaign against the coalition of Vercingetorix, following the very rapid capture of Vellaunodunum (7.11.1–2), Cenabum itself (7.11.7–9), and Noviodunum (7.13.2). Vellaunodunum fell in just three days and suffered very little except the confiscation of *matériel* and hostages. Caesar admits (7.11.3) he is in a rush to move on to Cenabum, where the killing of Romans had begun the recent trouble. And yet, having captured the *oppidum* with little trouble, Caesar rushes through the aftermath and says nothing about taking revenge. The violence, as often in Caesar, is markedly succinct: *Oppidum dīripit atque incendit, praedam mīlitibus dōnat*" ("he sacks and burns the town, gifts the plunder to the soldiers" 7.11.9). An overt reference to revenge for the slain Romans at Cenabum, who were themselves the victims of a sort of Gallic *dīreptiō*, is wholly absent. Instead, that lust for vengeance is carried forward, beyond the troublesome but rapid conquest of Noviodunum (7.13.2) and onto the set-piece siege of Avaricum.

The critical phrase in Caesar's account which reveals the cause behind this seemingly misplaced violence is "*et Cenabī caede et labōre operis incitātī*" ([the soldiers] spurred on due to the slaughter at Cenabum and the suffering of the siege work" 7.28.4). The murders at Cenabum could not be the sole justification for the massacre at Avaricum because Cenabum itself was subjected to a much more common, and much less organized, destruction. Rather, at Avaricum the fervor for vengeance mixes with Roman *labor operis*, the fever pitch brought on by the burden of their suffering. At this point in the campaign, the scorched-earth tactics of Vercingetorix have crippled Roman foraging, their allies have struggled to provide supplies, and the legions are starving. The siege of Avaricum has dragged on far longer than the quick capturing of Vellaunodunum, Cenabum, and Noviodunum: the war at Avaricum has literally bogged down, and it seems plausible that Caesar's response was overwhelming brutality. Violent and wrathful responses to a long or difficult siege are found elsewhere in Roman history: the wholesale slaughter at Masada during the Judaean revolt, for example.[5] Caesar utilizes the lengthy and elaborate struggle at Avaricum to exemplify the singular focus and endurance of his soldiers, his own mastery over violence in the face of adversity or the enticements of *dīreptiō*, and the Roman guarantee of ultimate (if misplaced) revenge.

---

[5] Josephus, *War of the Jews* 7.8-9

GLOSSARY

This list contains: (1) the 250 most commonly occurring words in Latin, drawn from the Dickinson College Commentaries Latin Core Vocabulary, which also appear in the text of this book; (2) other words which appear frequently in the text

ab/ā: away from; by (prep. + abl)
absum, abesse, āfuī, āfutūrus: be away, be absent
ac: and, and also, and besides
accidō, accidere, accidī: happen, occur, take place (frequently impersonal)
accipiō, accipere, accēpī, acceptus: receive, get; take
addūcō, addūcere, addūxī, adductus: bring/lead to; prompt, induce, persuade, incite
adeō, adīre, adiī, aditus: go to, approach
adventus, adventūs m.: arrival, approach
ager, agrī m.: farm; field; land
agger, aggeris m.: siege ramp, siege mound
agō, agere, ēgī, āctus: drive, lead; do; act
aliquis, aliquid: someone, something
alius, alia, aliud: some, other; another
alter, altera, alterum: the other (of two)
altus, -a, -um: high; deep
amīcus, amīcī m.: friend
animadvertō, -vertere, -vertī, -versus: notice, observe; discern
animus, animī m.: soul, spirit, mind; (in pl.) high spirits, courage
annus, annī m.: year
anteā: before, earlier, formerly
antecēdō, -cēdere, antecessī: go before, precede; excel, surpass
apud (prep. + acc): among, in the presence of
arma, armōrum n.: weapons, military equipment
artus, arta, artum: narrow
at: but; but indeed
audiō, audīre, audīvī, audītus: hear, listen to

aut: or; either...or

autem: however; moreover; also**bellum, bellī n.**: war

beneficium, beneficiī n.: kindness, favor, benefit, service

cadō, cadere, cecidī, cāsūrus: fall; die

capiō, capere, cēpī, captus: take, capture, seize, get

caput, capitis n.: head; leader; life

castra, castrōrum n.: soldiers' camp; fort

causa, causae f.: cause, reason; case, situation; (+ gen) on account of, for the sake of

cēdō, cēdere, cessī, cessus: go, move (typically with a prefix in Caes.)

celeriter: swiftly, rapidly

centuriō, centuriōnis m.: a commander of a *centuria*, about 80 men in the time of *Gallic War*

certus, certa, certum: definite, sure, reliable

cīvitās, cīvitātis f.: (in Caes.) a tribe, community; (elsewhere) state, citizenship

clāmor, clāmōris m.: loud shout; noise, uproar

coepī, coepisse, coeptus (only perf.): began, undertook

cognōscō, cognōscere, cognōvī, cognitus: learn, recognize; (in perf.) know

cōgo, cōgere, coēgī, coāctus: drive together, bring together; force, compel

comittō, comittere, -mīsī, -missus: bring together, join; engage; entrust

commūnis, commūne: common, general, of/for the community

concēdō, concēdere, concessī, concessus: yield, grant

concilium, conciliī n.: council, discussion

cōnferō, cōnferre, cōntulī, cōllātus: bring together, compare; bestow; (with *sē*) take oneself to, go

cōnsilium, cōnsiliī n.: counsel, advice, judgment; plan, purpose

cōnstituō, -ere, cōnstituī, cōnstitūtus: place, station; arrange; decide; halt

cōnsūmō, -sūmere, -sūmpsī, -sūmptus: use up, spend; destroy

contineō, continēre, continuī, contentus: hold together, bound, restrain

contingō, contingere, contigī, contāctus: touch, adjoin, border on

cōpia, cōpiae f.: ample supply, plenty; (in pl.) troops, forces

cunīculus, cunīculī m.: tunnel, hole, mineshaft

dēbeō, dēbēre, dēbuī, dēbitus: ought, must, should

dēdūcō, dēdūcere, dēdūxī, dēductus: lead down/away; win over; withdraw

dēfendō, dēfendere, dēfendī, dēfensus: guard, protect, cover; support
dēsistō, dēsistere, dēstitī, dēstitus: leave off, cease, desist from
dīcō, dīcere, dīxī, dictus: say, name, designate
diēs, diēī m./f.: day
difficultās, difficultātis f.: difficulty, trouble, distress
discēdō, -cēdere, -cessī, -cessus: depart, withdraw; scatter; abandon
dō, dare, dedī, datus: give
domus, domūs f.: home
doceō, docēre, docuī, doctus: make aware, teach, inform
dūcō, dūcere, dūxī, ductus: lead, command; consider
dum: while, as long as, until; provided that
duo, duae, duo: two
ēdūcō, ēdūcere, ēdūxī, ēductus: lead out; draw up
eō: to there, to that place
eō, īre, iī / īvī, itus: go
eques, equitis, m.: horseman, cavalryman, rider
equitātus, equitātūs m.: calvary
equus, equī m.: horse
et: and
ex/ē: out of (prep. + abl)
exercitus, exercitūs m.: army
exīstimō, -āre, -āvī, -ātus: think, consider; judge
facilis, facile: easy, simple
faciō, facere, fēcī, factus: do, make
fāma, fāmae: report, rumor; public opinion; reputation, fame
ferē: nearly, almost
ferō, ferre, tulī, lātus: carry, bear; endure; report
fidēs, fideī f.: faith, loyalty; pledged word; protection
fīnis, fīnis m./f.: boundary, end, limit, goal; (pl.) country, territory
fīō, fierī, factus: occur, happen; become, be made, be done
flūmen, flūminis n.: river
fortūna, fortūnae f.: chance, fate; prosperity; condition, wealth
frūmentārius, -a, -um: relating to provisions or supplies, esp. grain

frūmentum, frūmentī n.: grain; crop
fuga, fugae f.: flight, escape
gerō, gerere, gessī, gestus: carry; manage, conduct, perform; wage
genus, generis n.: type; kind
habeō, habēre, habuī, habitus: have, hold; consider
hic, haec, hoc: this; these
homō, hominis m.: man, human being, person
hortor, hortārī, hortātus: urge, incite, cheer, exhort
hostis, hostis m.: enemy
iam: now, already, soon
ibi: there; in that place or time
īdem, eadem, idem: the same
ignis, ignis m.: fire
ille, illa, illud: that; those
imperium, imperiī n.: command; authority
imperō, -āre, -āvī, -ātus: give a command, order; rule, control
incendō, -ere, -ī, -sus: set on fire, burn; incite
initium, initiī n.: beginning
inopia, -ae f.: lack, need; poverty
īnstituō, -ere, -ī, -tus: begin; arrange, set up, prepare; decide, determine
intellegō, -ere, intellēxī, intellēctus: know, discern; understand
inter (prep. + acc): between, among
interficiō, interficere, interfēcī, interfectus: kill, destroy
interim: meanwhile, in the meantime; however, nevertheless
ipse, ipsa, ipsum: himself/herself/itself (intensive pronoun)
ita: thus, so; therefore
itaque: and so, therefore
iter, itineris n.: journey; road; passage, path
iubeō, iubēre, iussī, iussus: order, command
labor, labōris m.: effort, exertion, work; suffering, distress, hardship
labōrō (1): labor; suffer
lēgātus, lēgātī m.: (of Romans) lieutenant, legate; commander; (of others) ambassador, messenger, representative

legiō, legiōnis f.: legion, army
levis, leve: light, thin, trivial, trifling, slight; gentle; fickle, capricious
lībertās, lībertātis f.: freedom
locus, locī m.: place, location (plural is neuter)
magis: more, to a greater extent; rather
magnus, -a, -um: large, great
malus, -a, -um: bad
manus, manūs f.: hand; team, gang, band of soldiers
medius, media, medium: middle, middle of
mīles, mīlitis m.: soldier
mīlle, mīlia: thousand
mittō, mittere, mīsī, missus: send
moveō, movēre, mōvī, mōtus: move, stir, set in motion; disturb
multitūdō, multitudinis f.: crowd, mob; large amount
multus, -a, -um: much, many
mūrus, mūrī m.: wall
nam (conj.): for
nātūra, nātūrae f.: nature, the natural word; quality, property
neglegō, neglegere, neglēxī, neglēctus: disregard, neglect; despise
nec (conj.): nor; and not
neque: nor; and not; neither…nor
nisi: if not; except, unless
noster, nostra, nostrum: our; (in pl.) our men, i.e. Roman soldiers
nox, noctis f.: night
nūllus, nūlla, nūllum (gen *nullīus*): no, none, not any
nūntiō, -āre, -āvī, -ātus: announce, report
obses, obsidis m./f.: hostage
omnis, omne: every, all
opera, operae f.: work, effort; trouble (cf. *opus*)
oppidum, oppidī n.: town; stronghold, fortified place
oppugnātiō, oppugnātiōnis f.: attack, assault; siege
opus, operis n.: work, task; construction, defense (cf. *opera*)
palūs, palūdis f.: swamp, marsh

parō, -āre, -āvī, -ātus: prepare; furnish, supply
pars, partis f.: a part, share, portion
pater, patris m.: father
paulō: a small amount, a little; somewhat
per (prep. + acc): through; during; by means of; on the pretext of
perīculum, perīculī n.: danger
perterreō, -ēre, —, -itus: terrify thoroughly
perveniō, -īre, -vēnī, perventus: come to, arrive at, reach; approach
pēs, pedis m.: foot
petō, petere, petīvī, petītus: seek; ask for, beg for; attack
pōnō, pōnere, posuī, positus: put, place, set; station
porta, portae f.: gate (of a town)
possum, posse, potuī: be able
post (prep + acc): behind; after
post: afterwards, after
praesidium, praesidiī n.: protection; help; guard
premō, premere, pressī, pressus: press, press hard; pursue; overwhelm
prīmus, prīma, prīmum: first, chief, best; nearest/next
princeps, principis: foremost, leading; (as subst.) influential individual
prō (prep. + abl): in front of, before; on behalf of; in return for; instead of
prope (prep. + acc): near
prōdūcō, -ere, -dūxī, -ductus: lead forward, bring out, reveal
proelium, proeliī n.: battle
profectus: see *proficiscor*
proficīscor, proficīscī, profectus: set out, depart, commence, march
prohibeō, -ēre, -uī, -itus: hinder, restrain; forbid, prevent
prōvincia, prōvinciae f.: a territory outside of Italy, governed by a Roman official; in *Gallic War* it typically refers to *Gallia Trānsalpīna*, later called *Gallia Narbōnensis*, the narrow coastal strip of southern Gaul which connected Italy to the Spains (see Introduction map)
putō, -āre, -āvī, -ātus: think, suppose; reckon
quidem: indeed (postpositive), certainly, even, at least; (*ne...quidem*) not...even
quisque quaeque, quidque: each

quō: (to) where

ratiō, ratiōnis f.: account, report, statement; matter

recipiō, recipere, recēpī, receptus: take back, regain; receive, admit

redūcō, redūcere, redūxī, reductus: lead back; withdraw; restore

relinquō, relinquere, relīquī, relictus: leave behind, abandon

reliquus, reliqua, reliquum: remaining, left over

rēs, reī f.: thing; event, business, affair

saxum, saxī n.: a stone

sed: but

semper: always

sīc: thus, so

signum, signī n.: signal, sign; military standard, banner

silentium, silentiī n.: silence

sine (prep. + abl): without

singulī, singulae, singula: single, separate, one at a time, individual

soleō, solēre, solitus: be in the habit of; be accustomed to

spatium, spatiī n.: space, distance; extent

stō, stāre, stetī, status: stand, stand firm

sum, esse, fuī, futūrus: be, exist

summus, summa, summum: uppermost, highest, topmost; (partitive) top of

tamen: yet, nevertheless, still

tantus, tanta, tantum: such, of such size; so great

tempus, temporis n.: time

tertius, tertia, tertium: the third

timēns, timentis: fearful, afraid

tōtus, tōta, tōtum: the whole, entire, total

trabs, trabis f.: a wooden beam; timber

trādō, trādere, trādidī, trāditus: hand over, deliver; surrender; betray

trānseō, trānsīre, trānsiī, trānsitus: go across; pass by, pass through

tum: then, next; at that time

turris, turris f.: tower; a moveable siege machine

ubi: when; where

ūnus, ūna, ūnum: one

urbs, urbis f.: city

veniō, veīre, vēnī, ventus: come

versus: turned in the direction of, towards, facing

via, viae f.: road, path, route

victōria, victōriae f.: victory

videō, vidēre, vīdī, vīsus: see, look at; (in pass.) seem, appear; seem good

vincō, vincere, vīcī, victus: conquer, defeat

vir, virī m.: man

virtūs, virtūtis f.: strength, vigor, bravery, courage, excellence

vīta, vītae f.: life

volō, velle, voluī: wish, want

vōx, vōcis f.: voice; utterance

www.ingramcontent.com/pod-product-compliance
Lightning Source LLC
LaVergne TN
LVHW010623100826
845148LV00014B/3078

* 9 7 8 1 7 3 7 0 3 3 0 3 5 *